A THOUSAND
SMALL SPARROWS

A THOUSAND SMALL SPARROWS

Not One Is Forgotten

AMAZING STORIES *of*
KIDS HELPING KIDS

JEFF LEELAND

WITH MARCUS BROTHERTON

MULTNOMAH
BOOKS

A THOUSAND SMALL SPARROWS
PUBLISHED BY MULTNOMAH BOOKS
12265 Oracle Boulevard, Suite 200
Colorado Springs, Colorado 80921
A division of Random House Inc.

All Scripture quotations, unless otherwise indicated, are taken from the Holy
Bible, New International Version®. NIV®. Copyright © 1973, 1978, 1984 by
International Bible Society. Used by permission of Zondervan Publishing House.
All rights reserved. Scripture quotations marked (KJV) are taken from the King
James Version.

With permission, some names and other specifics have been changed for various
reasons.

ISBN 978-1-59052-933-1

Library of Congress Cataloging-in-Publication Data
Leeland, Jeff.
    A thousand small sparrows / by Jeff Leeland with Marcus Brotherton.—1st ed.
        p. cm.
    ISBN 978-1-59052-933-1
    1. Children—Diseases—Case studies. 2. Medical social work—Case studies.
I. Brotherton, Marcus. II. Title.
    RC58.L384 2007
    618.92—dc22

                                                                    2007006399

Printed in the United States of America
2007—First Edition
10 9 8 7 6 5 4 3 2 1

This book is dedicated to all the children who are Sparrows. Your courage to face medical challenges with simple faith and hope in God is a gift to many others. You inspire us to exchange self-pity for compassion, self-protection for courage, self-indulgence for character, and self-absorption for good conscience. You have helped us learn to love.

CONTENTS

SPARROWS OF SELFLESSNESS

SPARROWS OF DIRECTION

SPARROWS OF PURPOSE

SPARROWS OF TRIUMPH

SPARROWS OF JOY

All the stories in A Thousand Small Sparrows *are true.*

ACKNOWLEDGMENTS

You have in your hands a collection of heartfelt stories from many wonderful people. A very special thank-you to the children, teens, parents, teachers, and volunteers who have been involved in Sparrow Clubs and have shared their journeys with us in these pages. We are grateful as well to our special friends at Multnomah Books who have made this book project a labor of love to help advance the mission of Sparrow Clubs USA.

A Thousand
Small Sparrows

How Sparrow Clubs Work

Kids Can Do Heroic Things...

When They Have Heroic Things to Do

S parrow Clubs USA is a cutting-edge national youth charity where kids help other kids in medical crisis by doing good for their communities.

Sparrow Clubs USA actually helps two types of kids: children in medical need and everyday youth who long for something purposeful to do, whether they realize it or not.

Young people need sanctuary in their world today—safe places where they can release their compassion, courage, character, and conscience by learning to care for one another.

Sparrow Clubs USA gives them this opportunity and shows that kids can do heroic things...when they have heroic things to do. Here's how it works:

1. Children (and their families) in medical and financial crisis are referred to Sparrow Clubs USA by schools, social workers, parents, and doctors.

2. Children are adopted by area Sparrow Clubs and become "Sparrows." Sparrow projects are held in elementary, middle, and high schools; colleges; youth groups; service clubs; youth ranches; and more. Sparrow Clubs USA provides all-school assemblies, workshops, club handbooks, and tools for kids. Kids often meet their Sparrows in person. The clubs do community service projects and fund-raising events to benefit their adopted Sparrows. Clubs can get as creative as they want in encouraging and supporting their adopted Sparrow children and families.

3. Local businesses or individuals provide seed money by sponsoring a club for each adopted Sparrow. The area clubs "earn" the funds provided by the sponsoring businesses or individuals by doing community service projects. Money is then credited to a Sparrow family up to ten dollars per hour of service. Each Sparrow has a designated tax-exempt project account that is administered by the Sparrow Clubs USA nonprofit organization. One hundred percent of the "Sparrow Cash" and additional monies raised are designated to the Sparrow's account. A Sparrow family can access the cash for medical needs or for family needs incurred by their child's medical condition.

I pray that God would fill your heart with dreams,
And that faith gives you the courage to dare to do great things.
—Mark Harris, "Find Your Wings"

An Unexpected Hope

Are not five sparrows sold for two pennies? Yet not one of them is forgotten by God. Indeed, the very hairs of your head are all numbered. Don't be afraid; you are worth more than many sparrows.

Luke 12:6–7

We learn to recognize hope in unexpected places, sometimes even better when we're in a place where we don't have any hope at all. My family was in that place once. Hope visited us at a very low time, in a very unexpected way. Today that hope has expanded into a vision that is greater and more far reaching than anyone could have dared imagine.

On August 19, 1991, my fourth child, Michael, was born. That same day I was offered a job as teacher and activities director at Kamiakin Junior High near Seattle—a cross-state move for my family.

Six months after the move, Michael became sick. He was diagnosed with a rare form of leukemia. A bone marrow transplant was needed to save his life. But because I had changed insurance carriers with my new job, my new son fell under a twelve-month waiting period for transplant benefits. Our six-year-old daughter, Amy, was a rare perfect donor match. But Michael was disqualified for the $200,000 procedure that could spare his tiny life.

How does a teacher come up with $200,000?

My income was already spread thin supporting my family of six. I had taken another job selling encyclopedias part-time just to cover the higher costs of moving to a bigger city. Medical bills not covered by insurance began to swamp us. Our baby had fallen through a narrow yet deadly crack in our nation's health-care system. We appealed to the insurance company, to the state, and in quiet brokenness, to God.

LIVING IN A HOLDING PATTERN

Life continued, in spite of the waiting.

As the new PE teacher at Kamiakin, I was "stuck" with the job of taking Mrs. Kennedy's self-contained special ed class one hour a day. It was called Adaptive PE. The class consisted of twelve disabled kids—three in wheelchairs, two with Down syndrome, a couple with autism, and the rest with a variety of other physical and mental disabilities. We played simple, makeshift sports and games, a far cry from the Advanced Conditioning classes I typically taught, which were filled with jocks. But Adaptive PE quickly grew on me. These kids displayed an amazing depth of character—from courage to face challenges greater than I had ever imagined, to unrestrained joy in even the most minor successes, to an unhindered expression of love and appreciation that ministered…yes, mostly to me. These kids possessed a poignant realness and innocence seldom seen in today's junior high schools.

That spring, my baby boy, Michael, was hospitalized several times with infections and fevers. I spent many sleepless nights by his bedside at Seattle's Children's Hospital. Exhausted, I'd head back to school each morning. My wife, Kristi, would replace me for the day shift.

Many days I'd arrive at school sulking in self-pity. I'd survive until fifth period—Adaptive PE. Then my world would change again. The Down syndrome kids, Ben and Heather, would greet me with a familiar and refreshing hug as I entered the classroom. Smiles and waves would come from the rest of the kids. The games would begin, and we'd always have a lot of fun. Danny would be smiling ear to ear, quite content to simply stretch his gnarled limbs on the gym mat, as he watched the others run and play. I'd see fun-loving Mike competing intensely with the muscular dystrophy that barely permitted his fingers to manipulate the motorized controls of his wheelchair—the clock winding down in his own battle for life.

The epiphany for me came as I began to see my own circumstances through the clarifying lens these students offered me. My ingratitude and self-pity dissipated—hope and strength dawned again in me… *I have a lot to be thankful for. Really—a lot!*

ONE HEROIC ACT OF KINDNESS

Second semester, a seventh grader named Dameon Sharkey transferred into Adaptive PE. Dameon was neither physically nor mentally disabled, but the school counselor placed him there because she thought it would be a safer place for him than regular PE. Dameon was physically overweight and emotionally undernourished at school—one of those walking wounded kids that youth culture tends to target. Probably dyslexic, Dameon had trouble reading and writing. He wore big black stretch slacks with a white button-down shirt and tie to school every day. He walked with a fused-ankle limp and sweated his way to school each morning. Dameon scored low on the popular culture curriculum in the hallways—brawn, beauty, brains, and bank accounts. He was an easy target for abuse.

Dameon seemed to feel safe in Adaptive PE. He called it "boot camp" and viewed himself as a helper. Immediately he took charge of pushing Danny in his wheelchair around the track when we did our warmup laps. Dameon soon became my right-hand man. He was a battle history buff and spent a lot of time at home watching war documentaries on TV. He could quote Winston Churchill with ease. His sense of humor, outlook on life, and keen observations of people never failed to keep the class smiling and intrigued. He even earned the leg press championship by lifting the whole stack in the weight room. We developed a cheer in the class, used for any kid who showed uncommon perseverance. I can still hear it today: *Hey, Dameon! Go, Dameon! Attaway! Attaway!*

But pressures from home were never far behind me. Three months after Michael's diagnosis, my wife and I received a devastating report. Our son's leukemia was now classified as "aggressive." Michael needed the transplant immediately. If he didn't get the transplant, he would die. We scrambled. We phoned. We pleaded our case to all the powers that existed. Still, the insurance company refused to cover costs.

Unbeknown to me, word about Michael was spreading through Kamiakin Junior High. Teachers found out first and began taking collections. One dropped off a $500 check at our home.

Then on Friday, May 15, about a month before school let out, I received a phone call from Dameon's mom, Barb Sharkey. Fifteen minutes later, in came Dameon to my office with his mom close behind.

"Mr. Leeland," Dameon said, "if your baby's in trouble, I'm going to help you out."

Reaching out his fist, Dameon placed twelve $5 bills into mine. Sixty dollars—it was Dameon's entire life savings. This boy who faced mountains of adversity in life had sold the farm to help me. Words can't describe how I felt at that moment. I just hugged Dameon and said, "You're the kind of guy I'd bring to the trenches with me."

Dameon walked out of my office as if he were twelve feet tall.

WHEN COMPASSION CATCHES FIRE

I was powerfully moved by Dameon's gift and immediately took the money and the story to Steve Mezich, our principal. He was inspired to open a bank account for Michael. That afternoon, the Michael Leeland Fund was seeded with Dameon's $60 of hope.

Funny how word spreads in a junior high school. Students, en masse, grabbed the baton from Dameon's hand and raced to the challenge. Ideas sprang from idealistic adolescents—like issuing a petition to boycott the multimillion-dollar insurance company. Others combined altruistic creativity and personal sacrifice—walkathons and raffles were held, donation boxes sprang up in every classroom. Compassion was unleashed in the hearts of kids.

Individual stories were always most touching to me: Mary cashed in $300 of savings bonds; Kristen stuffed $100 of savings in a classroom donation box; Jon, a student who was perpetually in trouble at school, proudly brought in $26 for Michael after knocking on neighborhood doors; the ninth-grade class donated the dance money that traditionally funded its year-end graduation party. A junior high school was taking on the impossible. They were winning, but there was still a long way to go, and the clock on Michael's life was ticking.

Then the Seattle media caught wind of the story. Newspapers and television news spread the word across the state. Each gift made a difference and tipped the scales in Michael's favor.

Insurance company employees donated money, even though their company, under contract, could not. An inmate at the Monroe Correctional Complex sent in $25. An unemployed man, $30,000 in debt, sent $10. A second-grade girl donated a bag of pennies from her broken piggy bank. A total stranger made the largest single gift of $10,000. An eighty-year-old man who still washed dishes for a living sent in one dollar.

In the eye of a hurricane of grace, we watched in stillness from Michael's bedside as the awesome power of love struck full fury against impossible odds. Miraculously, our immense financial barriers were blown away like dust. In less than four weeks after

Dameon's donation, the Michael Leeland Fund contained more than $227,000—more than enough to schedule the transplant.

Small Beginnings, Big Rewards

A few weeks later, our daughter Amy donated her bone marrow to save her little brother's life. The transplant was a success, our son's cancer went into remission, and today Michael is a happy and healthy, football-playing, amazing teen. He's more than a survivor; he's living proof that something good can be unleashed against despair. Michael's life is a constant reminder that each day is a gift. We thank the Lord for him.

That spring, back in 1992, Dameon was given the school's character award at the annual awards assembly. As he came forward, the entire gym full of students and teachers erupted in a standing ovation. After school that day, Dameon sauntered up to me and reported, "Hey, Mr. Leeland, you wouldn't believe all the girls who are talking to me now!"

Many Kamiakin Junior High students who were ninth graders during Michael's ordeal graduated in 1996 from Juanita High School. Their class magnetically attracted an unprecedented $1.1 million in scholarship money. Dameon graduated with honors two years later in a remedial track. He was awarded a $3,600 scholarship by PEMCO Insurance Company—sixty times $60. For the next two years he attended Seattle Central Community College. Dameon perfected a wonderful gift for woodworking and eventually became a cabinetmaker.

For several years, many of us who had experienced what happened at Kamiakin Junior High wrestled with another dilemma: Michael was certainly not the only sick child in America. Could what had happened at Kamiakin happen at other schools? In 1995 we launched Sparrow Clubs USA—a nonprofit, youth-based charity seeded from Michael's miracle fund. We started on a shoestring. There were no offices at first. We all had other jobs. We just knew we needed to create something that helped us all look beyond ourselves and set the stage for more heroic acts of kindness within schools. We truly believed that Sparrow Clubs could not only help families with children in medical crisis but also become a catalyst for positive change in the hearts of kids and youth culture.

Why name it Sparrow? The small creature outwardly illustrates how we as human beings often feel. Most of us fly unnoticed beneath the radar of worldly importance. We all struggle with feelings of purposelessness, powerlessness, and insignificance—especially young people. But Jesus says in the Bible that God does not let any of His creatures go unnoticed—even something as small as a sparrow. As the Author of all life and compassion, God notices our hurts and offers healing and hope to every outstretched hand.

Numb from Disbelief

Though I didn't see Dameon as much after he graduated, we would talk on the phone and e-mail regularly. He'd ask how Michael's health was, philosophize about life, and tell me about his next woodworking project.

When Sparrow Clubs was formed, Dameon became one of our key volunteers. He handcrafted items to raffle at fund-raising events. Sometimes he spoke at our events. Dameon had a soft spot for children in medical need and for kids who needed to heal by taking their eyes off themselves to help others.

Our family moved to central Oregon, and Dameon came to visit us. He came on the train and brought his prized ornate chess set. He taught Michael, now his little buddy, how to play. I could picture Dameon coming to work with Sparrow Clubs someday when we grew big enough to hire more staff.

But late that year, the unthinkable happened.

Dameon developed a staph infection from a leg injury sustained while woodworking. The infection quickly spread through his body and into his vital organs. He underwent emergency surgery.

Early morning, November 1, 2000, Dameon's mom phoned with the news that Dameon had died.

I was numb from disbelief.

We had lost our Dameon.

Next Saturday afternoon the chapel was packed for the memorial service. Dameon's parents asked me to officiate, something I was honored to do. It's hard to speak when you're grieving, but my feelings were overruled by a greater debt of love.

The service was homespun and straightforward—just as Dameon would've wanted. We played a CD of the *Peanuts* opening piano piece—a Dameon favorite. Family and friends shared their stories and cherished memories of him. I read a Bible passage that reflected Dameon's relationship with God. And finally, with his parents' permission, I showed a video interview I had taped of Dameon for Sparrow Clubs only weeks before. Seeing Dameon up on the video screen, a ray of joy momentarily burst through our tears.

It was a Dameon moment, pure and profound. In my heart, our Adaptive PE cheer echoed loud and clear: *Hey, Dameon! Go, Dameon! Attaway! Attaway!*

YOUR INVITATION TO HOPE

Dameon's inspiration sharpened and magnified my vision for the vital work that was fast becoming my life's calling. Just two months after Dameon departed for heaven, I left the security of my career to go full time as the first director of Sparrow Clubs USA.

Dameon once said to me a phrase that changed my life: "Kids need sanctuary in schools." Dameon's words became my mission. By adopting a Sparrow to a student body, we've discovered a subtle but very positive influence that can disarm the often troubled culture of an entire school. Kids are idealistic—they sense what could and should be. They have great passion and energy to face incredible odds. Sparrow Clubs invites youth to enter into the struggle of a little one in need and, in the process, also serve their community. The program is a very effective tool to help build character, courage, conscience, and compassion in students' lives everywhere.

Today, Sparrow Clubs USA has projects all across the nation, helping hundreds of sick children and their families.

But more than that—literally thousands of other kids have also been helped because they've been motivated to help make a difference.

From Dameon's initial gift of $60, an entire movement has been created—an entire movement of hope that helps people everywhere.

In the pages ahead, you'll meet people whose lives have been touched by Sparrow Clubs over the years. These are the voices of parents, volunteers, teachers, business leaders, advisors, club members, and Sparrow kids themselves. These are the voices of quiet heroes, voices of faith, hope, love, courage, and inspiration.

Some of the stories have happy endings, and some do not. Real life doesn't always deliver happy endings. But these Sparrow stories, in their authenticity, show us glimpses of real goodness beyond even the most painful chapters in our lives. They show help in action, the power that comes from service, and the inner fortitude of compassion, courage, conscience, and character.

Consider these stories as cups of cold, refreshing water—small tastes offered from the floodgates of heaven's hope.

Your invitation is to drink deeply.

Jeff Leeland

Executive Director, Sparrow Clubs USA

Bend, Oregon, September 2006

SPARROWS OF COURAGE

It makes me happy to see people happy.

We made them happy so much

they were crying.

—Sparrow Club Member, Elementary School Age

JACOB THE BOXER

J acob's face looked like it had gone twelve rounds. Bruised, bat-
tered, black-and-blue—this was no way for a newborn to spend
his first few moments in the world.

"Nine pounds, eight ounces," the scales read. The nurse repeated
the information. Lying on the birthing bed, Priscilla Jove could
hardly believe it. Her new son was huge—and he was three weeks
early. But what did it matter? Aside from the severe bruising, Jacob
checked out completely healthy. Her new son was perfect.

Priscilla had worried that maybe this pregnancy wouldn't be as
smooth as her first two. Labor had been quick this time—only forty-
five minutes. The drugs she had been given made pushing sudden
and harsh. Jacob fought his way out like a boxer. He arrived glorious,
wet, and triumphant, although a bit beat up. He would be tough,
just like his dad, Sean Jove.

That Priscilla and Sean were having children at all was a miracle. Years earlier, when the couple lived in Los Angeles, they had
been dubbed infertile. They had run the gamut of treatments. Hor-
mone shots just made Priscilla crazy. She took them anyway, but in
the end—after hot flashes, waiting, praying, hoping, money out the

door—still nothing. One day, in desperation, she fell on her hands and knees before God and turned it all over to Him.

"Lord," she said, "it has to be from You."

Two months later she was pregnant.

Priscilla got prepared. If pregnancy, birth, and child rearing were about being organized, she wanted to get an A-plus. She scoured bookstores, devouring everything she could find. She made lists. She planned. She sorted. The couple's first child, Sarah, was born right on schedule. Two years later, the details worked out perfectly again. Another daughter, Libby, arrived like clockwork.

The girls were bright, brilliant, beautiful. Priscilla and Sean were thrilled. Still, it felt like a member of the family was missing. Sean is a man's man. He works as an electrician, surrounded by an industry that prizes brawn and heft. Sean's father died when Sean was young. He knew what an incredible bond can exist between a father and a son. For Sean, having his own son would help heal that wound. Two years after Libby was born, Priscilla became pregnant with Jacob.

Their family would be complete.

When All Your Plans Change

For some reason, nothing about her third pregnancy seemed organized. Priscilla had cravings this time—not normal pregnancy cravings, but intense, acute cravings. Once, in the middle of the night, it *had* to be cereal and cold milk. But the milk couldn't be cool—it had to be *icy, crunchy*. She put the milk in the freezer before she ate the cereal.

A doctor confirmed that something was out of whack. Priscilla was diagnosed with gestational diabetes, a type of glucose imbalance that starts during pregnancy and affects about 4 percent of women. Priscilla knew the high sugar levels in her blood could be unhealthy for both her and her baby. If diabetes isn't treated, a baby can have problems at birth—usually nothing serious, maybe jaundice or low blood sugar, but occasionally a baby can weigh much more than normal. Priscilla took insulin shots. Doctors reassured her all would be well.

Aside from the bruising, Jacob was born perfect and stayed on course his first year of life. He was an active little guy, gurgling and cooing strong and true. His checkups all showed health and vigor. Other than a slight tremor in one hand, all was well. Whenever Jacob concentrated, trying to pick something up, his hand would give a little shake. Nothing big. But Mom and Dad kept a watchful eye on it.

Jacob learned to walk right on schedule. He'd plow along, all boy, pressing forward to whatever he could grab. Sometimes he'd stop suddenly. Not a normal stop—more a stunt-man stop. It was like someone pulled a cord on him, jerking him back. Never quite seeing it happen, Priscilla wondered if one of the girls had pushed him down, good-naturedly, as siblings can do. But they hadn't. No one was pushing him down.

One day, at a regular checkup, Priscilla relayed the news to her pediatrician hopefully, almost nonchalantly. This was nothing, wasn't it? The doctor's alarm caught Priscilla off guard. Jacob was scheduled for an emergency MRI the same day. He was rushed to the hospital and placed inside the giant horizontal tube for the test. But the MRI showed nothing. So Jacob went to a specialist. "Maybe a muscle disorder," came the reply. "He'll probably grow out of it." Priscilla wanted to believe that. She says now that she should have asked more questions then—way more questions.

One month after that first round, Priscilla knew Jake's condition involved something much greater than a muscle disorder. Always a boy, Jake reached into the kitchen trash one day at home and cut his finger on a can. It required a few stitches—all part of growing up. After a tetanus shot, though, the chaos began. Seizure after seizure racked Jacob's little body. Somehow the shot had acted as the tipping point for whatever had built up in his little system.

The seizures didn't stop.

For days, Jacob was in and out of the emergency room. Nothing worked. Sean took care of the girls while Priscilla drove Jacob the three hours from their home in Bend, Oregon, to one of the larger hospitals in Portland.

On the first trip into the hospital, Priscilla watched her nearly two-year-old son take beautiful tiny steps. Her walking son, still on target for a life of running, jumping, just being the boy they'd hoped he'd be.

Those were the last steps Jacob took.

JUST FOR TODAY

Hospitals can be helpful places. Supportive. Caring. Healing. Miraculous.

Hospitals can also be frustrating.

After four days, Jacob was discharged. Tests showed nothing, even though Priscilla now had to carry her son back to the car. Her mom joined her. They planned to stay at a friend's house for the night and drive back to Bend the next day. Thirty minutes from the hospital, on the long Interstate 205 bridge from Oregon to Washington, Jacob began having what are known as cluster seizures. With Jacob strapped in his car seat, Priscilla was unable to stop the car on the freeway bridge. They counted perhaps one hundred seizures, one right after another, blows landing on Jacob like the midrounds of a welterweight championship. Jacob screamed with each one. For a mother's ears, Priscilla said, it was unimaginable.

They raced back to the hospital, but policy said since Jacob had just been discharged, he needed to follow admittance procedures again. Priscilla took him to the emergency room to wait. With Jacob having seizures on the hospital floor, Priscilla reached the doctor—the same doctor who had examined her child less than an hour earlier—by phone.

"You have to help us!" she said.

"Sorry," the doctor said. "He's not my patient anymore."

Priscilla was livid. Jacob was given Valium in the emergency room. The family drove across the city to another hospital.

Says Priscilla of the experience: "He was never the same kid again."

Jacob spent ten days in the next hospital. He had spinal taps, full workups, any test any doctor could think of. All results came back the same: inconclusive diagnosis. On February 22, during that ten-day stint, Jacob celebrated his second birthday from his hospital bed.

"The hospital staff brought him a cake, which he couldn't eat, and a little Elmo doll—which made him smile," Priscilla said. "But it was just a yucky day."

So they came home.

Present day. For a woman who once needed to plan everything, Priscilla no longer considers herself a planner. For more than a year now, Jacob has had ups and downs, but mostly downs. For a while, Jacob still crawled. He doesn't crawl anymore. He has problems swallowing. He can't reach or grasp anymore. He no longer shows interest in toys. It's a progressive shutdown. The official diagnosis is "degenerative neuromuscular disorder of unknown origin." Translation: something's wrong; nobody knows what it is.

"Having a sick kid changes everything," Priscilla says. "I have no control. We went into survival mode. We just try to get through every day now."

One of the hardest parts is simply not knowing the future. Jacob has had such medical lows that his parents have planned his funeral twice. There are still doctor visits and neurologist visits and specialist visits. They recently visited the Mayo Clinic in Minnesota, hoping for something concrete there. They found nothing. Some have even ventured to say that Jacob will outgrow this. But Priscilla says the family has held on to that belief for too long.

Some bright moments exist. Priscilla says everyday activities take on new meaning. Going to the grocery store, taking a walk with Sarah and Libby—she doesn't take these things lightly. Priscilla and Sean's marriage is tighter than it's ever been. Jacob's illness has made the couple go deep.

Small Hope, Small Brightness

Sparrow Clubs was held at Sarah's elementary school the year before Jacob got sick. It took Priscilla awhile to fill out a reference form for Jacob because she was in such an emotional place. She didn't want her daughters' schools to be the host school for Jacob. If he didn't make it, then her daughters would forever be known as "the sisters of that kid who died." So Jacob was paired with a high school. The kids did penny drives and talent shows to raise money. Priscilla e-mailed the school with updates.

Christmas 2005 was the hardest time—but also the most poignant. Priscilla had always baked, decorated, made Christmas a big deal for her family, but this year she couldn't. This Christmas felt neither joyous nor happy; it was just about getting through.

Somehow the kids at the high school found out. They arranged for a Santa to come to the house with gifts for everyone in the family. There were homemade crocheted scarves, toys for the kids, relaxation candles for the grownups—the Joves' garage was literally full of presents. Everybody in the family was bawling. Somehow the tears helped.

"We were really feeling like we were going down," Priscilla says of Christmas that year. "But they helped it be the best ever for our kids."

Life continues for the Jove family. The hardest part is just not knowing what will happen.

Jacob has a new neurologist and more tests scheduled. The last one had simply told the family to keep Jacob comfortable until he dies.

But nobody accepts that.

"We're still fighting," Priscilla says. "If they don't know what it is, then how do they know there's no help available? We're not giving up."

SAMI SOARS

Samantha Dulley long-eyed the violin like a carpenter peering down the length of a board. She marked its balance and straightness, its color and feel. Her sixth-grade band teacher had just handed the instrument to her. Sami wanted to play it so badly. She wanted to take the bow in her hands and climb, climb—learn to scale heights and peaks, ascending, circling, wheeling, flying. A violin could make her soar.

"I'm not sure if that will work for you," her teacher said at last.

Sami had tried. Her brain knew what to do. It told her so: Grab that violin and put it under your chin, Sami. Hold it steady. Just hold it steady. That's all you need to do.

Her body seldom listened to her brain.

The violin shook. Her hands shook. Her chin shook. She… just…couldn't…seem…to…hold…that…wonderful…stupid… violin…steady…enough…

Sami put it down. She knew she would never play it.

JUST AN EVERYDAY KID

"It's hard to walk and talk and do normal things," said Sami, when asked to describe what life's like with cerebral palsy. "But I want people to know that our minds work good."

Five years have passed since Sami tried to play the violin. At seventeen, she's a junior in a regular high school. It's just before lunchtime, and in about ten minutes, Sami will join her friends in the cafeteria. She hopes it's pizza day, her favorite. Taco day is all right too. But not hamburger day. The cafeteria never seems to get hamburgers right.

"I don't remember my first surgery," Sami said. "I think it was to straighten out a bone in my leg." Her words come out clearly but slowly, with a slight slur. She's shy, warm; every once in a while she laughs the brightest, most self-assured chuckle. She's had six surgeries in all.

"I used to get teased a lot in elementary school," she said. "When I walk, I drag both feet. And when I eat, I can't shut my mouth because of my muscles. I want to, but I just can't."

Sami has always gone to regular schools. She's had special education helpers in most classes. This year she has two high school mentors to help her—Jessica and Ashley—some of her best friends ever, Sami said.

Junior high was actually easier for her than elementary school. The kids knew her by then. It felt like they understood her better. It took more work to walk between classes, but she didn't need as much help with her schoolwork.

High school is probably most fun, she said. She likes English, math, and ice cream. She hangs out with her friends at her church's youth group. She dances to music on her CD player at home—mostly oldies, rock 'n' roll, some hip-hop.

One of the best things about high school, but sort of embarrassing, too, she said, is that she's a bit of a celebrity now. It's hard to walk down the halls without someone saying, "Hi, how are you?" Since seventh grade, Sami has been a Sparrow. She was the girl everyone rallied around and raised money to help. The kids have all grown up together now. They've helped her, and she's helped them.

At first, her friends raised money to get her a wheelchair. Sami can walk, but it's always better to ride for long distances. She was able to borrow a wheelchair at school but couldn't take it home. Besides, it didn't fit right and was uncomfortable to use for a long period of time.

So her friends special ordered a wheelchair for Sami. This one is a lot nicer. It has a backrest and fits her body. A few years after that, extra money was used to give her a walker. Sometimes Sami needs to sit down for a while when she's heading to classes. This walker has a bench built in—perfect for getting your breath back.

"I think it's amazing that the kids did it," Sami said. "They reached their goals, and what they did gave me a lot more mobility with the wheelchair. With the walker, I can be more free."

Sami noticed something else changed when she became a Sparrow. Kids had a different attitude around her. The teasing all but stopped. Kids were willing to help out, to be involved, to care.

"Kids tell me they learned how to help others in need," Sami said.

WHEN YOU LEARN TO FLY

When her fellow classmates gave Sami her wheelchair, they held an assembly just for her. They had worked hard to raise the money. The principal brought in a motivational youth speaker, a rock climber who had been injured and became a paraplegic. As an object lesson, the climber had rigged ropes and pulleys to the gym's ceiling. He asked Sami if she was willing to try something new. Sami agreed.

The gym was packed with five hundred middle schoolers, and Sami was strapped into a harness. She lay on her stomach, stretched out on a gurney-type device—the kind you'd see underneath a hang glider. Up, up she went, hoisted halfway to the ceiling. All the kids were on their feet by now, stomping on the bleachers, crazy with clapping, hoarse from cheering.

And in that harness, Sami flew. She climbed and climbed, scaled heights and peaks, ascending, circling, wheeling around and around the gym, celebrating what everyone had done. For one glorious moment, she was a kite, a bird, a banner flying over the entire school.

"It was a bit embarrassing," Sami said later. But she laughed, too, as she told the story, and smiled. This memory will be with her forever.

Next year Sami will graduate from high school. She plans to attend community college for two years, then transfer to a university.

Her goal is to become a special education teacher, working with second graders mostly, she hopes.

"I know I've got a challenge ahead of me," Sami said. "The work will be difficult, but I'll get through. I never really think about having cerebral palsy. It's just like 'whatever.' I've got better things to look forward to in life."

After lunch in the cafeteria today comes band practice. Sami never did learn to play violin. But her sixth-grade teacher suggested she try the cello instead. It's a bigger instrument and rests on the floor. You don't have to hold it under your chin—that makes it a bit easier to play when everything shakes. Today, Sami's a star in her high school orchestra.

And when she plays the cello, she soars.

Moments

How much time does it take for a life to completely change? A year? A month? An hour? A second? How fragile the security we think is present in our lives.

For parents Rhonda and Jay Scheresky, life zipped along at a brisk pace but always seemed quite normal—as normal as can be with two active little boys, Nicholas, four, and Alex, almost two. Moments revolved around toy dump trucks and sandboxes, running and jumping, two little guys just growing up vibrant.

Each day now takes on new meaning.

- July 1. Home. Just life as usual. Rhonda is three and a half months pregnant with the couple's third child. She's a bit tired but feeling good overall.

- July 2. On a trip to ride the Thomas the Tank Engine tourist train in Hood River, Oregon, Rhonda notices a spot on Alex's leg. It looks like a pimple, but it's redder, darker, almost like a spider bite. Alex has a great time on the train, but he tires easily. He's not himself.

- July 3. Alex has a fever. He rarely gets sick. Maybe he's just worn out from the trip. That night two more spots appear, one on his chest, the other on his back.

- July 4. Alex has a fever still. Regular doctor offices are closed for Independence Day. Rhonda takes Alex to the emergency room. "This is no infected spider bite," the on-call pediatrician says. He's an oncology specialist. He rushes Alex in for tests. Blood tests show that Alex's white blood cell count is unusually low. More tests are ordered.

- July 5. Cultures are taken of the spots on Alex's body. Results show bacterial growth one would normally find in a swimming pool or lake. Usually a healthy body can fight this off. For some reason, Alex can't.

- July 6. Alex is sent on the three-hour drive to a hospital in Portland for a bone marrow biopsy. He arrives late in the afternoon. It's a teaching hospital, and Rhonda finds it unnerving to have so many medical students hovering about her son.

- July 7. A biopsy is performed. Fortunately Alex is put out for the procedure, as it's painful. The doctor's conclusion comes quickly and certain: acute lymphoblastic leukemia, cancer of the bone marrow, the most common type of leukemia in children. The doctor tells it like it is, Rhonda says, which the family appreciates. Still, Rhonda and Jay are devastated.

- July 8. Morning. Alex has surgery to have a port implanted in his chest. Medicine can be administered more easily that way. After surgery, that same day, Alex receives his first round of chemotherapy. He is twenty-two months old.

In one week, from July 1 to July 8, the Schereskys' world has completely changed.

CHANGE IN MOMENTS

Three weeks after his first round of chemo, Alex stops walking. Rhonda had tried to prepare herself for it—the doctor said it would happen—but no amount of groundwork readies a person for this. Her child had just learned to walk, finding his first steps. Those steps, it appeared, might have been his last. Overwhelming.

"I think his age helps," Rhonda says. "I don't think he understands what's going on."

The good news—the hopeful news—is that this form of cancer is *usually* treatable. Survival rates are high, very high, particularly if the family can reach the three-year mark. Alex's treatment has just begun, so that's still three years away. First on deck: spinal taps once a week for five weeks. The couple drives weekly between central Oregon and Portland.

At home, Rhonda and Jay learn to administer antibiotics to their son three times daily, once at 6:00 a.m., the next at 2:00 p.m., the final at 10:00 p.m. Each treatment takes thirty minutes. Fortunately, Alex is napping or sleeping at those times. The treatments leave him exhausted anyway. Mom or Dad handles the portable IV pump, the syringes and saline and medicines. They learn how to flush the IV line and how to hook up and disconnect tubes. Jay works long hours as a police officer. He takes a lot of time off work, but most treatments fall to Rhonda. Now midpregnancy, she's exhausted and emotionally drained.

Summer is missed. Fall begins, and the hardest part of Alex's treatment is behind them. Alex gains more strength despite the treatments and finds himself more energetic, more like his old self. He starts walking again. Still, there's a huge fear of the unknown. Always around the corner is another day, another possibility that something will take a turn for the worse. Once, Alex's port gets flipped, making it impossible to access, and he needs another surgery to right it. Another time Alex gets an intestinal infection and has to go to the hospital for six days. Basically the child has zero immune system. He's constantly at risk of infection and can't be around anybody. This means Mom can't go out either. Isolation sets in. The family feels quarantined. "August to December was a complete roller coaster," Rhonda says.

Change comes again in October. This time, it all happens in less than twenty-four hours.

Rhonda's mother is her best friend. She has been there through everything. Rhonda's dad passed away fourteen years earlier, and Rhonda became exceptionally close to her mother after that. Rhonda's mom is virtually the only baby-sitter for Alex after he becomes sick. But she's much more than that.

- October 17, 11:00 a.m.: Rhonda receives a phone call from her stepdad. Mom's gone to the hospital with a brain hemorrhage. Very sudden. Very unexpected. It doesn't look good.

- 3:30 p.m.: doctors say the damage is irreparable. A decision is made to pull Rhonda's mom off life-support. Rhonda comes back to the house to administer Alex's chemo.

- October 18, 2:00 a.m.: Rhonda's mother dies in the hospital. She was fifty-eight.

Rhonda doesn't sleep for the next seventy-two hours. Why her mom? Why this? Why this *now*?

MOMENTS OF HOPE

That fall, Alex is connected with a Seven Peaks School in Bend, OR to become their Sparrow. Alex can go out of the house by now, as long as no one around him is sick and he wears a mask, so the family gets to meet the kids at school. They give Alex a huge basket of stuffed animals, which delights him. For one of the few times since Alex got sick, Rhonda feels a twinge of encouragement.

"It was such a change after all the isolation," Rhonda says, "to see firsthand and know somebody was with us in this. Alex is so little. It's amazing to see the impact of what he's dealing with."

An assembly is held. Red Robin restaurant becomes Alex's business sponsor and brings its mascot to the assembly. Alex goes and enjoys meeting the big bird. School parents sign up to deliver a free Red Robin meal to the family each Friday evening.

Then it was like a dam broke, Rhonda says. And the outpouring of gifts and encouragement washed over the family with full, glorious force:

- A girl wins a bicycle from a fire department contest, takes it back, and exchanges it for one Alex's size.
- Another young volunteer puts a jar in a grocery store. Pennies, please. She raises $150 for Alex.
- One six-year-old gives her entire life savings to Alex—$41 carefully stuffed away in a cigar box.

- Several kids donate *all* their Christmas gifts to Alex, or in the case of one child, what her parents would have spent on her Christmas presents—$150.
- A boy gets his father, a construction company owner, to take Alex for a ride in some of the company equipment. Alex rides in a semi truck, a cement truck, a front loader, and a track hoe. A kid who loves trucks, Alex never wants to leave the job site.
- Kids come over and rake pine needles at the Schereskys' house.
- The art club raises $75 by making calendars and selling them along with ceramic pins.
- Sparrow Clubs throws Rhonda a baby shower for the new arrival.

"It's so encouraging to see selflessness in kids so young," Rhonda says. "My son may be ill, but he's making a difference in their lives. It works both ways."

On December 28, the Schereskys' third son is born—a quick induced labor because the Schereskys need to juggle the day. Alex is between courses of chemo and is feeling okay for the moment. A neighbor comes over while Rhonda gives birth. Jay comes home to look after Alex and Nicholas. Rhonda comes home with their new baby brother, Samuel.

For the moment, the family celebrates.

April now, and Alex is in the maintenance phase of his treatments. He has two and a half years to go before he's pronounced cured. He still receives oral chemo daily and injections once a month, but the doses are lower this time. His immune system is up, and he can play with other kids again, as long as they're not sick. His hair has grown back. He looks like a normal, healthy little boy again.

"So far it's a happy ending," Rhonda says. "He was once a very sick little boy, and so far he's getting better. We know our life is in God's hands. That's our real security."

How much time does it take for a life to completely change? A year? A month? An hour? A second? How strong the Security that we know is ultimately in control.

ONE CALL

One phone call can change everything. It can strike at any time, and your life will change—radically, ceaselessly, irreparably.

Matt Jacobson received such a call more than six years ago. His new publishing company was just getting off the ground. Hours were long; money was stretched. His wife, Lisa, was pregnant with their fifth child. All previous pregnancies and births had been normal, uneventful, wonderful. Expectations for this pregnancy were the same.

Then the call. Matt was at work. Lisa, at thirty-six weeks, was on track to give birth in another month. That morning she had gone in for a routine checkup. She called from the doctor's office. Her voice sounded strained, urgent.

"Matt…the doctor says we need to induce labor—right now!"

One call.

Everything changes.

AND THE PARENTS SAID "AMEN"

Matt rushed to the hospital. The alarm seemed to have lessened by the time he arrived. Doctors sounded routine—"Everything is fine"—they just felt they needed to take the baby sooner than expected. Lisa was started on Pitocin, a drug that induces labor. Hours went by. Doctors ordered a C-section.

After the baby was lifted out, Matt and Lisa were able to kiss their new child—a little girl they named Avonléa. Doctors said, "We've got some things we need to look into"…and Avonléa was whisked away. That was it. Matt stayed with Lisa while she was sewn up. They felt bewildered, happy the pregnancy was over, but definitely puzzled. What was going on?

The doctor who told them was straightforward yet gentle. Avonléa had suffered a massive stroke before she was born. The stroke took most of the left side of her brain and wiped out much of the right side as well. Matt and Lisa asked a litany of questions. The doctor's answers had an ominous sameness:

"Will she ever walk?"

"No, probably not."

"Will she ever talk?"

"No, probably not."

"Will she ever see?"

"No, probably not."

And so on…

When the doctor left, the gravity of the situation crashed over

Matt and Lisa. "We suddenly realized we were going to have a vege-table for a child," Matt says. "All our hopes and dreams for her were washed away."

The couple wept together. They allowed themselves one long moment of raw grief. Then they steeled themselves with what they knew to be true. There, in the hospital room, they spoke to each other about God's sovereignty: One Personal Cause has all dominion over everything. That Personal Cause is always good. *God is good*—one simple yet amazingly complex truth. This was their opportunity to embrace what they had believed only theoretically until then. Matt got on his knees beside his wife's bed, and the couple prayed.

"God, we don't understand this, but we're confident You do." Still in prayer, they made a decision. From that moment on—no matter what happened, no matter what life held or didn't hold for Avonléa—they determined to give their child as much as they could. Always.

And the parents said *Amen*.

Rafts of tests were ordered over the next days. Doctors, thera-pists, and developmental specialists assessed activity. Normal brain activity shows up electrically on a monitor as a series of sequential bumps. Avonléa's looked like erratic scribbling. Her limbs were almost completely flaccid, no muscle tone, no spark. Her arms were splayed. She offered no reaction—no clasp, not even a twinge of awareness—when a foot or hand was touched. Tests showed that her brain was full of blood.

The first month in the hospital slipped by. Doctors wanted to diminish all brain activity in an effort to help Avonléa's brain heal. Eye and ear patches were ordered to reduce stimulation. Massive numbers of wires and tubes kept bodily functions working—she looked like a science experiment, Matt says, a little pot of spaghetti. Lisa fed Avonléa breast milk through an eyedropper. No one was allowed to touch her.

"There is no greater feeling of helplessness for a parent than when you can do nothing for your child," Matt says. "It's intensely frustrating. You can't fight. There was nothing to do except keep our hands off."

Matt and Lisa lived at the hospital for two months. Matt's mom, Patricia Jacobson, quit her job and looked after the other children. The stress and sleep deprivation for Matt and Lisa was overwhelming, but it was only beginning. Avonléa was sent home, not because she was well, but because the hospital had done all it could do.

At home, Avonléa needed to be hooked to a breathing and heart-rate monitor each night. If the baby's heart stopped or if she stopped breathing, an alarm would sound, and the parents would have to rush to her side before she died and get her heart started or get her breathing again. Doctors showed them several techniques.

In any household, if a child's heart stops just once—or if a child stops breathing—it's a huge deal. What does a parent go through if her child stops breathing? What is it like for a parent to try to restart his child's heart?

Picture it. For eighteen months, Avonléa's monitor never went off fewer than five times each night. The alarm averaged twelve times nightly. Regularly there were nights when it went off as many as forty-five times.

"It was just torture," Matt says. "We could barely function."

A REAL SUNBEAM

When you go through a life-altering experience, you typically do not think as rationally as you might otherwise. Matt says that if all his faculties had been functioning during that dark season, his pride would have gotten in the way when others offered to help. He's glad now that his pride took a backseat.

Within two years of Avonléa's birth, medical bills ballooned. On top of that were countless overnight stays at hospitals, involving hotels, meals, and gas. Thousands of dollars spent on medical equipment were not covered by insurance. Matt had just started a business. The family wasn't rich by any means, but because they owned their house, they weren't able to qualify for assistance. The bills rolled in.

From out of the blue, Sparrow Clubs USA called. A representative had found out about the Jacobsons through a friend of a friend. The club offered to adopt Avonléa as a Sparrow. Matt had no idea what to expect. He simply agreed.

Another call.

Everything changes.

"It was just amazing," Matt said. "You have so much to deal with emotionally; it's just an unspeakable blessing to have this one aspect of intense pressure relieved."

Matt says one of the difficult parts of receiving was that kindness came from so many sources. There was no way he could ever say thank you. He found it humbling. He discovered a wordless gratefulness he never knew existed. He did, however, express himself to the whole community in a letter to the editor for publication in the community newspaper:

> There is a standard, given long ago, for the governance of everyone's actions in the community—"Do unto others as you would have them do unto you." Lisa and I would like to extend our deepest gratitude to the students of Sisters High School, who through the Sparrow Club's first event, made a tremendously profound statement to us and the community. You reached beyond the confines and comfort of your own world into the life of a little one too weak to be her own advocate....

Help aside, daily, nightly, moment-by-moment battles for Avonléa's life continued. She threw up everything, so she had an operation that prevented vomiting. Once, her shunt got clogged. With a six-hour window to save her life, the family rushed Avonléa to the best children's hospital, three hours away. Upon arrival, Avonléa had major brain surgery within the hour.

Matt and Lisa helped their older children understand by continually telling them, "Avonléa is a special little girl."

One day in the car, the two older kids, both under eight, were able to have a candid discussion with their parents. The kids tried to get a better grasp of the specifics of what "special" meant.

"One thing it means is that Avonléa probably won't ever be able to walk or talk," Matt explained gently.

Savoury, the older girl, burst into tears. "Well, that's not very *special*!" she said.

Sometimes Matt and Lisa wondered too. It's hard for anyone to grasp the implications of a long-term medical experience for a family. People sometimes asked them how they did it. Or even asked questions the family found insensitive—like, "Is your daughter better yet?"

Better? What does that mean?

"How do we do it?" Matt says. "I don't know. God never gives you the grace for someone else's trial. He only gives you the grace to walk through your own. We have grace."

One form of grace comes from Matt's mom, Patricia. Her granddaughter is her personal project. Five days a week, four to five hours per day, she works with Avonléa, massaging and moving the little girl's body and providing visual and auditory stimuli. Patricia volunteered. She considers it an honor to have a hand in this little life's development.

Another form of grace comes from the rest of the Jacobson family itself. Despite all the difficulties surrounding Avonléa, the Jacobsons decided to have more children. Today they have eight: Britain, twelve; Savoury, eleven; Vienna, nine; Cambria, seven; Avonléa, six; Revere, four; Dauntless, twenty-one months; and

Hakon, four weeks. Big households often provide the best environments for special needs children, experts say. Matt and Lisa agree.

"Avonléa's in a household where children make her part of the group," Matt says. "There's always laughter and tears. She never sits in a corner by herself. She's always in a stimulation-rich environment."

And Avonléa has responded.

Today, this same little girl who was once considered to have close to zero brain activity is anything but a vegetable. She can hold a fork and feed herself and talk and carry on conversations. Whatever the rest of the family is doing, Avonléa wants to do the same—she plays with blocks, she folds clothes, she's into everything. Avonléa has 75 percent of her vision. Her family believes she will one day read and write. She can hear acutely, and tests show she has the cognitive level of a three-year-old—not bad considering she started from so far behind. Doctors say she has "far outstripped" any prognosis. She's come so far that doctors make no relationship between the initial prognosis and how Avonléa is doing today.

Avonléa has hazel green eyes and light brown hair. She has fair skin and a beautiful smile. She recently lost a tooth. She's not out of the woods completely—she has scoliosis and tilts to one side. Her muscle tone is improving but still needs some work. Matt and Lisa aren't worried. For today, as every day, they plan to keep doing what they've been doing. God is a good God, and the future looks clear.

"Avonléa's a bright, happy child," Matt says. "She's a real sunbeam. We're happy she's part of our family."

ALEX IS IMPORTANT HERE

His knock is quiet yet as determined as oak. Every Friday, seven-year-old Alex Baldwin goes door to door to each teacher's classroom at his school, picking up plants that need water. A special education assistant helps him, but not too much. Alex is confident enough now that he can go into classrooms alone. He pushes a little cart along, gathering the plants and taking them back to a station for water. The plants sit over the weekend. Then on Monday, Alex retraces his steps and hands the plants back to the teachers for the week.

Alex is in a good place now, a safe place. Things need Alex to care for them. And Alex is proud of his accomplishments. But the journey that brought him here should never have happened.

MEET OUR SON

Shannon and Matt Baldwin of Salem knew they wanted to adopt another child to be a brother or sister for their first adopted child, a little girl, McKenzie. Competition is fierce in the private adoption route. Everyone wants perfect babies. But the Baldwins' goal was simply to be parents again. The state foster care system is full of children needing adoption. After a child is three or four, his chances of ever getting a permanent home go way down. McKenzie came from foster care, and she had been a breeze.

The paperwork to adopt Alex had all been done ahead of time. Matt and Shannon knew a bit about him, but not much. That's okay, they reasoned. They were prepared to love him no matter what. They met him at a foster home several hours north. Alex, then almost four, came running out the door to greet them. Matt played football with him. Shannon gave him a fuzzy lion toy. It took about a week for the paperwork to clear, and they brought Alex home to a big party.

Alex was immediately so different from McKenzie. Was that simply because Alex is a boy? At first, the Baldwins thought he might just be color-blind—he couldn't learn his reds, greens, and blues. His speech wasn't where it needed to be either, but he had been housed in a Hispanic foster home, so surely it was just Alex transitioning to English. Alex was active, quite active, and several day-care situations didn't work for him. Shannon decided to quit her job and be a stay-at-home mom. The family traded their new cars for used ones and sold their larger house for a smaller one.

More than a year went by, and Alex began kindergarten. Once he was surrounded by other children, it quickly became clear that Alex was developmentally nowhere near his age group. Everyone sensed this—including Alex. He began to not want to go to school. Sometimes he threw tantrums and kicked things over. School staff labeled him an aggressive child.

The Baldwins weren't convinced. They took Alex for a variety of tests. Diagnoses by the dozen were suggested, but none quite fit. Mostly, all the doctors could agree upon was that Alex's case was "really complex." The Baldwins took matters into their own hands and began to research Alex's background. Turnover can be high in the state foster care system. Often reports and papers get misplaced. The Baldwins dug through files, placed phone call after phone call, located relatives, and even sorted through police files.

What they found out about their son astounded them.

What the Dents Meant

Alex, who is Hispanic, had been born into a gang. His birth parents were both members and were in jail. When Alex was placed in the foster care system, other gang members sought to get him back in honor of his birth parents. They harassed the first foster parents, throwing bricks and slashing tires, until Alex was moved to another foster home, then another, then another. Finally, he lived with an aunt, a single mother who had fled the gang system and only wanted what was best for Alex. That's when the Baldwins adopted him. The aunt was able to direct the Baldwins to other sources that helped fill in the rest of the story.

When Alex's birth father was arrested, there had been a domestic disturbance in the home. The father had tried to punch the mother but had ended up striking Alex instead. To this day, Alex has indentations in his head. His teeth are also broken.

After the birth father went to prison, the birth mother continued to neglect and abuse the child. The Baldwins had always wondered about some scars on Alex's head. His scars came from being slashed with a broken beer bottle.

The final straw was when Alex was locked out of the home one day. Passersby called police after seeing a toddler wandering in the middle of a busy intersection crying. Alex was naked from the waist down and covered in feces. The mother was found at home, passed out from drugs. Alex was two years, eleven months old.

Knowing how Alex became injured was one thing. Knowing the extent of how Alex's injuries would affect him would be another.

After the Baldwins had adopted him, in the middle of the night, June 2004, Alex suffered a severe seizure, cause unknown. A helicopter rushed him to a larger hospital in a nearby city. Matt flew with Alex. Shannon, who followed in a car, remembers speeding up on the freeway to ninety miles per hour, convinced she would never see her son alive again.

The seizure passed. No other symptoms were present, so Alex was released. He came back home and entered first grade that September. He did okay for a few months, but never very well. School stressed him. He began not sleeping. Sometimes he'd run away from school. He cried a lot. The school seemed to view him as an inconvenience, Shannon said.

By December that year, Alex was clearly going downhill. He began having problems with the simplest tasks. He couldn't figure out how to open doors anymore. The Baldwins took him to the hospital. Alex ended up staying there for five months. He was put on a medication for Parkinson's disease. Slowly Alex recovered. Doctors ran more tests. The first solid diagnosis came. From the injuries Alex suffered before he was adopted, his condition now stands as such: "traumatic brain injury, with mental retardation." Most people's intelligence quotient is about 100–110. Alex's IQ tested at 56.

WHEN YOU WEAR RED

The Baldwins knew they needed to make some serious life changes to be able to care for their son. First thing on the agenda was finding a school system that would welcome him. They researched options and located the Three Rivers K–8 public school in Bend, Oregon. Matt, who works as a police officer, applied for a job in Bend. The couple sold their house and moved.

The first meeting with school administrators was amazing, Shannon said. "By then, we were just exhausted and heartbroken." School administrators listened to the Baldwins' story with tears in their eyes. "They welcomed us to the school and told us everything was going to be okay. From moment one, they focused on Alex's positives."

Alex *did* have positives, despite his many setbacks. Alex has a very sweet disposition. He absolutely adores his older sister. He loves his grandparents. If he thinks anyone is in need, Alex wants to help. One of his regular chores is taking care of the family pets—two dogs and two cats. Alex gets their food and water and continually checks up on them. The cats, Jagen and Baxter, are his favorites. Alex made up Jagen's name. Both cats sleep in his room.

At his new school, Alex began to blossom. He went from snippets of a sweet disposition to that being his prominent characteristic.

Soon he started coming home from school smiling, laughing, telling his parents about his day, wanting to go back.

Early in their first year at the new school, the family got connected with Sparrow Clubs through the school's principal. She wanted the rest of the school to know about Alex and embrace him. Alex became a Sparrow and the school opened its arms. Older students would stop off at the house, inviting Alex to come play soccer and basketball. Fund-raisers were held. The community became involved. Alex recently went out for an ice-cream cone with his family. The clerk said: "Hey, I know you—you're our Sparrow." And Alex got another scoop for free. He beamed all the way home.

The prognosis for Alex is mixed. Academically he hasn't progressed very far this year. He has problems with his alphabet still, and counting is a chore. But everyone is hopeful.

"Alex's confidence is through the roof," Shannon said. "He used to say, 'No one likes me.' Now he says, 'Everybody loves me.' He's just so proud."

Shannon and Matt say they would do it all again, despite the challenges. Still, they want people to realize the one sad fact of Alex's story: his condition was preventable. "It never should have happened," Shannon said. "It makes me sad to think of the potential that was lost."

Still, there's a silver lining to every cloud. The Baldwins know their son's life has touched so many people already—including themselves.

"We never would have become the people we are without him,"

Shannon said. "He teaches people how to have compassion, patience, and love."

This blessing was seen soon after Alex was adopted by the Sparrow program. The school was holding its annual carnival—it wasn't a fund-raiser for Alex, just a fun event for everybody. Almost as a sidelight, someone asked Alex his favorite color, then suggested that the main carnival color that year should be red—Alex's color—in honor of their new Sparrow. Maybe people could even wear red clothes too, someone said. Posters went up around school.

On the evening of the carnival, the Baldwins arrived at the school's gym a bit late. "It doesn't take too much to get us crying anymore," Shannon said. When the family opened the front doors to the gym, they saw red everywhere. Red balloons, red streamers, red tablecloths. Red shirts, red pants, red jackets. Parents, teachers, students, community members—everyone was wearing red.

"This is for Alex," somebody whispered to them. "We want you to know he's important here."

Sparrows of Hope

I felt like a very, very glorious butterfly. It felt so nice to help.... I felt like somebody that I've never thought I've been before.

—Sparrow Club Member, Elementary School Age

Our Angel in Disguise

For some, Wal-Mart makes an unlikely heaven on earth—all that stuff just crammed under one roof. Wal-Mart means shelves of toilet paper, automobile tires, deodorant, bananas. It's fluorescent lights, canned music, and white floors.

But five-year-old Peter Burson loves the bustle.

The best day ever combines a trip to Wal-Mart with a stop-off at McDonald's—sometimes even the McDonald's located *in* the Wal-Mart. Two legendary institutions that know how to have a good time located under the same roof: it doesn't get any better than that.

Peter's favorite food is a McDonald's double cheeseburger—plain—with a Diet Coke. No fries. "Me-cheeseburger," said with a grin, is Peter's phrase that pays. Peter's mom and dad, Susan and Craig, know what that means. Eight-year-old brother, Samuel, is always up for lunch too.

That's what makes Peter happiest: the whole family all together, eating cheeseburgers at Wal-Mart. Peter likes it when no one's missing.

For a five-year-old boy with a penchant for simple family fun, it's a day that reflects something of the divine.

WHEN YOUR CRY IS A WAIL

Nothing showed up abnormal in Susan's pregnancy with Peter. He was born healthy; the future looked bright. Before he turned one, Peter would scoot but not crawl or walk. Well, some kids just do that—don't they?

The first clue came when Peter banged his head on the floor one day. He banged hard. It wasn't just curious noisemaking or body play either. This was insistent behavior. He didn't bruise or draw blood, but the banging was on his frontal lobes, purposely, almost as if he wanted to hit a certain part of his head.

Susan and Craig had previously experienced developmental issues with their firstborn, Samuel. Samuel had been born blind—cataracts—but he got lens implants and was seeing now. The wise parents knew something was up. They took Peter in for tests.

The first diagnosis came back broad based—"developmental delay." Now what exactly did that mean? Susan works for a urologist and is not intimidated by medical sidestepping. She pushed for better answers while the clock ticked. Peter had always been on the chunky side. Doctors speculated that he might have some sort of eating disorder—perhaps Prader-Willi syndrome, a life-threatening condition in which children develop insatiable appetites and often-dangerous obesity. By the time Peter was five, he weighed ninety pounds.

Peter endured more tests, and eating disorders were ruled out. But a gastrointestinal x-ray revealed another clue: Peter's liver and spleen were bigger than they should have been. Back to the metabolic doctor. Tests were sent to a lab in South Carolina. This time the diagnosis came back confirmed: Hunter syndrome.

Hunter syndrome is a rare disorder in which a child lacks an important enzyme that breaks down food and toxins in the body. As a result, the toxins build up in various tissues and organs and cause an assortment of damages. Hunter syndrome only affects males, typically between the ages of two and four. Complications include progressive mental retardation, aggressive behavior, hyperactivity, joint stiffness, deafness, enlarged heads, and enlarged internal organs. Survival for boys with severe forms of the disease is about ten to twenty years.

For Susan and Craig, hearing the diagnosis felt like someone had taken a brick and smashed their faces with it. Susan remembers driving back home from the doctor. Before Samuel was born, she had had a miscarriage. The feeling of mourning was similar, she said— just the same acute sense of loss. From somewhere deep within her, alone in the car, came an indescribable wail.

JUST LIVING TODAY

With some diseases, you can do something. You go and fight. With others, all you can do is let it unfold. You go home to wait.

Peter's diagnosis has been about waiting. His health has been relatively good. He's not on any medications, although he tires very easily. But he can walk and play for up to twenty minutes before needing to sit and rest. Playing with trucks is one of his favorite activities. Peter goes outside with his big brother to play with 4 x 4s.

They race their Big Wheel bikes together in the front yard. When Peter gets tired, they come inside and play with puzzles and blocks. A good evening involves eating ice cream and watching a video. *Annie* is Peter's favorite. He likes all the singing and dancing.

Part of the degenerative disease means that Peter's cognitive ability is affected over time. His attention span has become shorter. He can become very combative. He hits a lot, said his mom. Some days he hits everybody, including himself. Often he insists on calling others by wrong names, although he knows better. Some days, when you look into his eyes, it's like the lights are on, but nobody's home.

The toughest part is that the disease is always hanging over the family's heads. It's always there. "I know he'll go to heaven and be with the Lord," Susan said, "but there's still a void. It's the constant fact that my son will go home early—that's what's hardest."

Peter was recently linked up with an elementary school for the Sparrow program. It's still early in the process—things are just getting underway. The school recently held an assembly where Peter came and shook hands with all the kids. Despite his sometimes aggressive behavior, Peter loves kids. It was great to see compassion on all those faces, Susan said—the other kids *felt* something because of Peter.

"At times like those I'm reminded that I'm really honored to be Peter's mother," Susan said. "God has chosen Craig and I—for what reason I don't know, but the Lord will give us all the tools we need to endure this. Sometimes my faith doesn't look like much, but if I lean on the Lord, it is stronger."

OUR ANGEL IN DISGUISE

There is no cure for Hunter syndrome, but scientists are studying an experimental treatment called enzyme replacement therapy, which Peter is undergoing. It may stop the disease from getting worse.

In the meantime, there is today.

Today Susan had a cold: sniffling and sneezing, achy head, runny nose. This afternoon Peter came up to his mother, his eyes filled with compassion, and kissed her gently on the hand, to make things better.

"Me pray for you," Peter said.

Susan looked at her angel, his face filled with faith. This small boy, so on loan from above for this moment and the next, hopefully another tomorrow, another moment. For this moment, "it was like the countenance of the Lord was on him," Susan said.

She nodded. "Yes, please pray for me, my son, my amazing son."

Peter straightened to his full height, taking the job seriously. Reverently, he cleared his throat. His prayer consisted of four words, interpreted by divine ears that need nothing more than a child's outstretched hands.

"Jesus loves you. Better!" Peter prayed.

And he went off to play.

And Susan, for this moment, felt better.

A NORMAL KID

Alec McCleary, thirteen, is just a normal kid.

He's going to be a freshman in high school this fall. He likes bowling, movies, and hanging out at the mall. He used to like playing video games—*Mario Kart* and *Zelda* were his favorites—but not as much now that he's older.

To look at him today, anyone would think he's just another healthy kid.

But it hasn't always been that way. Ask him about the past, and mostly he doesn't remember. That's one positive side effect of what he went through, said his parents, Mark and Tiffani. Sometimes it's merciful to forget.

JUST A NORMAL KID

Alec grew up healthy. He has two older sisters, Joslyn and Sophia, and two younger brothers, Spencer and Finley. He used to get headaches once in a while. Doesn't every kid? Sometimes the headaches were pretty bad—by the time he was eleven, Alec was getting them two or three times a week. As the years passed, the headaches became more intense. His uncle, a head and neck surgeon, encouraged his parents to have Alec checked out.

The news came like a whirlwind. One day Alec is fine. The next morning, the family finds out he's got a brain tumor. That evening, the family packs up the minivan and drives five hours to the nearest children's hospital. Alec has nine-hour brain surgery—80 percent of the tumor is sliced away. The other 20 percent—the part that surgeons can't reach with scalpels—will be attacked with radiation.

Brain surgery of this magnitude can land like a dropped piano. *Wham!* Alec wakes up a completely different kid. It takes at least five weeks before he responds to anything. After that Alec completely relearns how to walk, talk, even smile.

For five months, the family lives in a Ronald McDonald House near the hospital while Alec has daily radiation treatments for the first eight weeks. Dad, a contractor, commutes back home to work during the week. Complications set in, and Alec develops swelling and seizures. He has more surgery to relieve fluid buildup in his head and spine. Infections set in. He's in the intensive care unit for several weeks. Finally Alec is well enough to go home. The tumor is still in his brain, but it's no longer growing. Things look good for a year and a half.

Alec needs another brain surgery, but it won't be as severe, doctors say, because they can go in through the same pathways as last time. He shouldn't forget how to talk or walk this time.

The family makes a quick decision to go on vacation first. "It sounds funny," Tiffani said, "but when you have a sick kid, you have to make the most of every opportunity."

The family went to the beach and for a few short days just enjoyed being normal—they swam in the pool, splashed down water slides, and zoomed around go-cart tracks. Alec had his hair back by then, looked healthy, and felt fine.

After vacation, Alec had his surgery; again surgeons couldn't get all of the tumor.

Twelve rounds of chemo were scheduled—one a month for a year. Right now, he's got nine down with three more to go. Every month, family members drive back to the hospital, where Alec spends about a week. He sleeps through most of the treatments. Mom—or anybody Alec can convince to do it—gives him foot rubs. There have been complications, but mostly Alec's body seems to be responding well to treatments. He has a bit of numbness, but that's about it.

Alec has missed a lot of school during the past two years, but he's kept up as much as possible. Friends have been really helpful, he says. He's grown up with the same group of kids since kindergarten, so there's a lot of support.

Alec became a Sparrow at his school this past year. His mom hesitated at first because she wanted him to be as normal as possible. But she knew Alec would lose his hair and have that "steroid, puffy look," so it would be helpful for other kids to know what he's going through.

Alec was excited about being a Sparrow. The school organized a baseball "hit-a-thon." A dollar bought three hits. The farthest hit for a teacher won a lunch out. The farthest for a kid won an iPod.

The school also held an assembly for Alec. Alec said he "didn't feel weird about it at all." He got up with the microphone and welcomed the students in, cracking jokes and stuff. Kids responded well when they learned what he was going through. Most were like, "Hey, how can I help?"

What does the future hold?

No one quite knows. But Alec doesn't seem to mind—or at least doesn't let it show if he does.

"I'm just chillin'," he says, "just hangin' out—you know."

His mom agrees.

"We just keep him laughing more than anything," she says. "Live your life for the life you have and not for the one you don't."

ONE STEP AT A TIME

Ashley Rucker-Vieira, fourteen, likes drawing, swimming, and playing the clarinet. Ask her about starting high school this fall as a freshman, and she just sighs.

"Thanks for reminding me," Ashley says.

When she thinks longer about it, though, she says she's really not that frightened at the thought of starting ninth grade. It's just a new environment, that's all. She's okay with it. Looking forward to it even.

Things will be all right—one step at a time.

Ashley has Duchenne muscular dystrophy, one of more than forty types of muscular dystrophy. She was born with it. It's a degenerative disease that gradually destroys all muscles, including the heart and breathing muscles. Survival beyond a person's early thirties is rare.

Ashley's parents, Joan and Dave, didn't find out their daughter had the disease until she was five. Before that, she ate normally, walked, crawled, got mad at her big brother—all the stuff little kids do. But at preschool they noticed she was having trouble keeping up with her peers. Running was a problem. She couldn't go up steps as quickly. It seemed she was always lagging behind. A pediatrician said she was just developing more slowly. He recommended orthopedic shoes. Further tests showed it was much more.

Prognosis is uncertain with this disease. This particular type of MD usually affects boys—only a handful of other girls across the country have it, so exactly how it will unwind in Ashley's life isn't well understood. The family has to wait and see. In the meantime, there is today.

A LONG, SLOW ROAD

For quite a while Ashley showed hardly any symptoms. She looked healthy. She attended all her classes. Muscle atrophy takes a long, slow road when doing its vice. At first, Ashley's walking started to slow. By second grade, she got tired a lot. Sometimes she used a wheelchair to get around at school.

Ashley doesn't remember it as a big deal when she started using a chair. She was too busy just being a kid. Every month, her school held a two-kilometer run. Students would push her in the chair. She'd zip along, arms out like an airplane, zooming along in the race.

In third and fourth grade, Ashley needed to use a wheelchair more and more. Walking felt unsteady, even short distances. She got knocked over easily. She began to use a wheelchair every day. Every six months, Ashley and her parents traveled about five hours to a children's hospital for physical therapy.

Over time, even pushing a wheelchair became tougher. Hills also are a bear. What Ashley really dreamed about was an electric wheelchair. An electric wheelchair means independence. And not just any old chair. Ashley's favorite color has always been purple. What would be really cool is a *purple* electric wheelchair. Now that would really take her places!

Electric wheelchairs are not cheap. The family looked into purchasing options. Insurance wouldn't cover the $15,000 needed. They considered selling their car. One day at school, Ashley voiced concerns to a friend. The next day the friend said: "You know, we need to do something about getting you a chair."

One conversation led to another. Word got around. The principal at the school knew about Sparrow Clubs. The ball got rolling.

"What made it cool," Joan said, "was that so many people wanted to help. From day one it was incredible. I can't even put it into words."

THE COLOR OF ELECTRIC

Ashley tends to be a quiet, shy kid. The attention of all her classmates doing fund-raisers for her proved to be overwhelming at first, she said. But she was thankful too. She never knew so many people cared.

That year, two days before Christmas, Ashley received her electric wheelchair. It was purple too! Students at her school raised all the money for it. Ashley drove it all over school as soon as the break was over. "Everybody was excited to see me in the wheelchair," Ashley said. "It was a pretty cool Christmas present."

Sparrow Clubs helped out other years too. A year later, Ashley needed glasses. Sparrow Clubs paid for them. Later she needed an adjustable bed. Sparrow Clubs raised the money for that too.

"Sparrows has been a godsend," Joan says. "We would have coped somehow, someway, but my goodness, it sure made life easier to be a part of it."

Ashley has become a bit of a celebrity. A television crew made a documentary about her for a character curriculum program. The DVD went all over the country. A teacher at the school, Jacqueline Taylor, wrote a book about her. The book's title—*Electric Purple*.

Ashley plans to graduate in a couple years, then go to college and study medicine. But for right now, there's a new high school to think about this fall. After that will come more drawing, more swimming, and more clarinet.

One step at a time, Ashley thinks to herself, *one step at a time.*

GOOD DAYS WILL COME AGAIN

J oel and Teresa Leard had two boys, Michael and Christopher, three years apart. Their family seemed complete. But five years later, something happened that would change their family forever.

Along came Megan.

What is it about a little girl's presence that can change a family so much? Instead of trucks and trains came dolls and daisies. And that was all Megan ever wanted to do: just be a little girl.

MEGASTRONG

Megan was a healthy and active child. One of her favorite activities was walking to the park with her dad. Every once in a while, Megan came down with a fever. Doesn't every kid? But in one week when Megan was seven, she seemed to get every flu symptom at once— including fever and even a bloody nose. Joel works in the medical field, and this was enough to spark his red-alert button. He and Teresa took Megan to the hospital. Tests confirmed their worst fear. This was no cold. It was acute lymphoblastic leukemia, considered one of the "best" types of leukemia to get (with an 80 percent survival rate) but cancer nonetheless. The family knew the going would be tough.

Rounds of procedures were launched immediately, including spinal taps and chemotherapy. Megan lost her hair within a week. A chest port was put in, then another, because the first one was put in incorrectly.

"It was hard on us as a family," Joel said. "Everyone was telling us this was an *easier* form of leukemia. None of it was easy."

Megan battled her disease for two years. She fought infections. She traveled to the hospital regularly. She took mounds of pills at home—steroids, oral chemotherapy, antinausea medication. Joel had never known how much was involved outside a hospital. Once Megan developed neutropenia—a blood disorder in which counts can suddenly become low. Joel said it was like watching a flower wilt before your eyes. One moment, Megan was sitting on the couch just talking normally. In the next moment she collapsed, as if the air had rushed out of a balloon.

"It was two years of peaks and valleys," Joel said. "Just really hard going for everyone."

During this time, Megan was adopted as a Sparrow by a middle school. Kids held car washes and other fund-raisers. For one fundraiser, the kids made wristbands with "Megastrong" printed on the side—a hybrid of Megan's name and how they saw her, as one tough cookie, able to go through anything.

"It was just an overwhelming response," Joel said. "The kids were amazing."

At age nine, Megan finished her treatments. Doctors began to use the word *remission*. Joel and Teresa breathed a sigh of relief, but never felt quite "out of the woods," they said. Megan looked good. Monthly checkups showed everything was healthy. A year went by, then two.

Then came a slightly abnormal lab report. Probably nothing. The test was done on a Friday; everyone said results could wait until Monday. But Joel and Teresa knew they couldn't. Tests came back with one word parents never want to hear: *relapse*. More leukemia, invasive this time, and in Megan's spinal fluid.

"The big question was 'Why?'" Joel said. "I couldn't understand it. We had done everything right. Doctors were so positive. It goes to show how little we know about things. I'm a doer, but there wasn't much I could do at this point. It was a real feeling of helplessness."

The same middle school readopted Megan as a Sparrow. Again came another overwhelming response.

And Megan fought on.

TWICE A SPARROW

Today, Megan, age eleven, is about three-quarters of the way through her second round of treatments. She's on an experimental drug and will start brain radiation in a few months. Doctors seem positive.

Megan still goes to the park with her dad, but their walks are shorter; Megan has slowed down a bit. She likes to read, crochet, and do things around the house. One of the hardest things is adjusting to being sick again, Joel said. "Megan just wants to be a normal kid again." For instance, Megan really likes swimming but can't always do that now because of her low energy level.

There are good moments too. Megan is all set to go to New York City this summer for a week. She'll go with the Sunshine Kids Foundation, a nonprofit organization dedicated to providing fun activities for kids with cancer. Activities are adjusted according to lower energy levels. Megan and a group of kids from the hospital will attend plays, go shopping, and visit the Empire State Building and the Statue of Liberty.

After that comes school again in the fall.

For now it's just one day after the next.

"On our good days, we just try to get out and stretch our legs and do something fun," Joel said. "That helps us on the bad days—to look back and remember the good and also to look forward and remember that good days will come again."

DEFINING FAITH

I n some cultures you name children what you hope they will
become.

Billy and Jenna Campbell named their first daughter Patience.
There were no lofty ambitions with the name initially. It came from
a line in an old lighter-waving rock 'n' roll anthem—"All we need
is just a little patience." But over time Billy and Jenna developed a
new appreciation for their daughter's name. Patience is endurance,
staying power, fortitude, serenity, a lack of complaint. It's a great
name to grow into. A great name for all parents.

Billy and Jenna named their second daughter Faith. They had
wanted it to be a middle name, but couldn't agree on a first name.
When the time came to write in a name on the birth certificate,
Faith was all they had. They had only an inkling of what the name
would foreshadow in their lives. Faith is confidence, trust, convic-
tion, assurance. Faith is what they would need now more than ever.

FOUR OPTIONS, NONE GREAT

Jenna and Billy went for an ultrasound when Jenna was twenty weeks
pregnant with Faith. Jenna stared straight at the screen, marveling at

the tiny blips of her daughter's image. She missed the look of alarm on the technician's face. But Billy caught it. The look flashed by in a moment. Nothing would ever be the same after that look.

Diagnoses came back firm and listlike. A hypoplastic left heart (where the left side of the heart—including the aorta, aortic valve, left ventricle, and mitral valve—is underdeveloped), a two-vessel umbilical cord (normally it has three), an underdeveloped bowel, and Jacobsen syndrome (a rare chromosomal disorder that tends to produce an additional list of problems, including facial, heart, and blood deformities). Only about 110 people worldwide have Jacobsen syndrome. Only about four people worldwide are living with this combination of Jacobsen and hypoplastic left heart syndrome.

Doctors said that Faith probably wouldn't make it. They gave Billy and Jenna four options:

1. Abortion.
2. Give birth, do nothing, take Faith home to die.
3. Roll the dice and put their daughter on the high-demand list for an infant heart transplant, knowing full well that the clock might run out before she could get a new heart. If she didn't receive the transplant, she would die.
4. Or have a three-stage surgery to repair her heart, hoping the surgery would fix the heart enough that it would last until she's twenty (when it's a bit easier to get a heart transplant) and/or also hoping that science will come up with some type of new procedure to fix her disorder by then.

Out of the four, option 4 meant the best chance for their daughter's survival.

But it would also mean a series of surgeries for their daughter. It would mean medications from here on out. It would mean the family spending huge seasons of their life at hospitals. It would mean endless traveling to clinics, endless phone calls with physicians, and bills, bills, bills, bills. It would mean the family would enter an unprecedented level of stress, for an unending amount of time, with no firm destination of health ever in sight.

The Campbells chose option 4.

Then it hit.

When Faith was five days old, she had her first surgery. Complications set in immediately. Her kidneys failed and major swelling was present. Meds were poured into Faith's tiny body. A breathing tube kept her alive for two weeks. For the first few months of her life, all spent in the hospital, the simple diagnosis was that Faith was not doing very well at all.

But Faith lived.

Faith was scheduled for her second stage surgery at age one, but she was deemed not in good enough shape medically. Surgery was the only option, so it was done anyway. Four days later, surgeons had to go back in to fix another problem. Then came a paralyzed right-side diaphragm, then a collapsed lung—three surgeries in all for the second round of surgery.

By this time Jenna and Billy could spout medical terminology as well as any health-care worker. Reading medical textbooks became as common as reading magazines. This was a lesson Jenna says she'd tell anybody with a sick child to learn as soon as possible—read up and take charge.

"You know your child," Jenna says. "I made the mistake of backing off a few times. But don't doubt yourself or set aside your intuition. Trust the warning signals you receive as a parent. Trust your gut, and speak up."

The constant worry hit Jenna the hardest. There were just so many ups and downs for a parent. One day her sinuses began to tingle. She thought it was just a cold, but her face went numb. She became confused and very slow. She thought it might have been a reaction to the antidepressants she had been taking. A few days later as she walked through the hospital, she noticed everyone looking at her strangely. The right side of her face had gone completely slack, her jaw and tongue shifted. Doctors thought she might be having a stroke, but they couldn't figure it out exactly. Jenna couldn't even say, "I'm not crazy."

It wasn't a stroke. For three weeks, Jenna's face drooped. Then her gut started to hurt. Whenever she ate anything, she'd double over in pain. Then came vomiting. She threw up for two weeks straight and lost twelve pounds. More tests were performed, and Jenna had gallbladder surgery—on Patience's birthday, of all days for a parent to need surgery.

More tests were performed; then a psychologist was called. The verdict? The unyielding stress was killing Jenna. A person can stand high levels of trauma for only so long before emotions emerge physically. At twenty-three, Jenna had the body of a fifty-year-old. She had constant acid reflux and gray hair. She was ordered to take a break. Billy's mom, Penny, took up the constant vigil in Faith's room.

Billy had his own problems. Insurance only covers so much—and the family had limited insurance to begin with. For a young family, this meant bills rolling in—and rolling right over them. Having enough money for food and rent became a concern. Collection agencies began to take money out of Billy's paycheck.

"She's Perfect to Me"

But dark futures have a way of becoming brighter—particularly with patience and faith.

Today, a good day for Faith, age one and a half, means learning how to walk. She can't quite stand unsupported yet but holds on to the couch and strolls along on her chunky feet, almost balancing, almost strong. She'll walk soon. Jenna and Billy know it. Patience, age three and a half, calls out encouragement to her younger sister. Patience has become an incredibly compassionate girl since her sister's birth. Patience has learned to be concerned for others—quite a feat for a three-year-old.

Faith is also quite proficient at playing the guitar. She'll prop herself up and strum her dad's. Sometimes she'll lay her head on the guitar as he plays. Friends bought Faith a toy guitar so she can make her own beautiful music. One of Faith's favorite songs is "You Are My Sunshine." Her mom sang it to her in the hospital room. Jenna sings it today to Faith at home.

"You are my sunshine, my only sunshine.
You make me happy when skies are gray.

You'll never know, dear, how much I love you.
*Please don't take my sunshine away."**

And Faith truly is their sunshine. "She's perfect to me," Jenna says. Billy agrees.

There will be more rounds of surgery to come. More tests. More procedures. More medical ups and downs. More teetertotter emotions for sure. There is no happy ending to the Campbells' story. They will never be out of the woods completely. But there are huge moments of joy along the way with two daughters named Patience and Faith. Isn't that what parenting is all about? Patience and faith—the characteristics all parents need. A full measure of each, pressed down, brimming over, spilling out for miles on either side. "If she lives to age forty, or just for a couple more days, we've had her for this long," Jenna says. "She's such a small child, but already she's touched so many people's lives for the good."

Touched lives she has. A group of high school kids in a nearby Sparrow Club sponsored Faith when she was still in the womb. They had never met or seen her—nobody had. The students just knew that a child was going to be born who would need help. They wanted to reach out.

After Faith was born, the child's precarious medical condition prevented the Campbell family from visiting the school for quite a while. Yet students kept on giving. Because of the medical complexities

---

* Lyrics excerpt from "You Are My Sunshine," words and music by Jimmie Davis and Charles Mitchell. Copyright © 1940 and 1977 by Peer International Corporation.

involved, Jenna had to give birth at a hospital three hours from the family home. Part of the money the students raised helped Billy take three weeks off work so he could be in the hospital with them. More support came after that. The kids did extra fund-raisers. They never let up. In all, over $18,000 was raised for Faith.

"We would have lost everything without Sparrow Clubs," Jenna says.

Students at Summit High School finally met their Sparrow more than a year after they had sponsored her. Something wordless had happened during the wait. Hearts and lives had been moved to action.

One of the high school girls, Elizabeth Voiles, wrote a poem about it. Elizabeth handed the poem to Jenna when she visited. Jenna cries when she tells the story today. The poem was written on flowered stationery with a custom font, cut out with stencil scissors and pasted on magenta construction paper. Jenna keeps it in a handy spot at home. The poem is as follows:

Defining Faith
by Elizabeth Voiles

What is faith to me?
Free-falling without the known facts,
    But feeling confident that you'll land on track.
Where do I find faith?
Around the world and over the seas,
    But most importantly inside of me.

Who is faith to me?
An infant so tiny that you must see,
    She was someone who needed someone like me.
When did I find faith?
When the moment was right,
    And the outlook wasn't bright.
Why is faith important to me?
Everyone needs a helping hand,
    And it's nice to have someone understand.

HOOP DREAMS

A t six feet tall, Gary Jackson's oldest daughter, Rosaunda, was basketball royalty. Just how good was she?

When Rosaunda (or "Ro-Ro," as she's called) was eight, she was considered one of the best child players in Oregon. She lived, ate, breathed, and slept basketball. As a high school freshman, she was five feet, eight inches tall and played varsity hoops for Jefferson High School, a strong basketball school. Ro-Ro played center and forward and was known regionally for her wicked shot blocks. Really, Ro-Ro could do anything she wanted on the basketball court. After playing three years for Jefferson, she transferred to Benson, one of the best basketball schools in the state, to play out her senior year. At Benson, Ro-Ro was classified the best basketball player to come along in nearly a decade. People believed she was Benson's hope for taking the state championship that year.

But all that would change.

WHEN A DIAGNOSIS DOESN'T COME

Just before Thanksgiving her senior year, Ro-Ro got a cold. This was a girl who never complained about anything, Gary said. It was more than sniffles. Ro-Ro wanted to stay home from school, something she never did. Two weeks later she was still lying around. She was walking strangely too, holding on to walls.

One Sunday, Ro-Ro stayed home from church while the rest of the family went. When they came back, Ro-Ro's tongue was swollen. They called the doctor. Soon Ro-Ro could hardly swallow. She was rushed to the hospital that night and was admitted immediately. Something was wrong—desperately wrong—but what?

Every test thinkable was thrown at Ro-Ro. Was it lupus? No. Was it cancer? No. All the doctors could do was treat her symptoms. Days passed, and Ro-Ro didn't get better. She got worse.

November turned into December turned into January. Ro-Ro stayed in the hospital. Her throat continued to close up. One day she quit breathing. A nurse caught it on a monitor and revived her. Ro-Ro lay lifeless in the intensive care unit for five days.

It was then, Gary said, that faith kicked in strong. The family— Gary, mom Sandra, and younger sister Celeste (Ce-Ce)—kept constant vigil around Ro-Ro's bed. They prayed, sang, and wrote out Bible verses on posters, taping them to the walls. Their favorite was "We can do all things through Christ who strengthens us." Prayer chains were started and spread across the country.

"I believe that's what brought her through," Gary says. "Faith— and her willingness to fight. She could have given up and died, but she chose to press on."

Soon all outside visitation had to be limited. Sandra stayed with her daughter round the clock for three months. Ce-Ce was always there. Gary kept working but came to the hospital every chance he got.

"That's the funny thing about this time," Gary said. "A lot of *good* came out of it. As a family we rallied and became closer than we had been since the girls were little. Our world was rocked, but the incident drew us together."

The Jacksons have faced more than one difficulty. Gary has had diabetes since he was twelve. When he and Sandra married in 1985, they knew the disease could cause a variety of problems over the years. Gary soon developed sight problems and later kidney problems. Today he is legally blind. He has about 1 percent vision on his left side. He can see his hand moving a couple of inches from his face, but that's it. The family has always coped with Gary's disabilities. And he has made the best of it. He works as a mortgage broker and is able to do many things.

But the family had never faced anything like this before.

WORSE BEFORE BETTER

For six months, Ro-Ro steadily declined. She lost control of her right hand. Her eyes would often go "crazy," Gary says. In March of that year, she made a slight improvement and went home in a wheelchair. She was able to walk again a bit, but one day she suddenly collapsed. Ro-Ro's legs simply would not move. The relapse landed her back in the hospital. More swelling was detected in her brain and spine. Ro-Ro lost control of her left side. She couldn't move her lower body.

Still, no diagnosis. Doctors called it some sort of name for insurance purposes, but no one knew for sure.

It was during that long season of darkness, Gary believes, that his daughter found her own faith. Ro-Ro had always gone to church, but the faith was more her parents', not hers. Month after month in the hospital, Ro-Ro began to call out to the Lord on her own. Others noticed the change. One doctor, known for his "stiff-collar" approach, began to spend more time in Ro-Ro's room just hanging out—sometimes he'd even take his breaks in there.

"I asked him why once," Gary says. "He said he just felt comfortable in there. The room had so much peace and love in it. He couldn't explain it."

Ro-Ro began to reach out to other patients as well. One boy had been paralyzed in an accident. Depressed, he didn't want to live. Ro-Ro went to his room to talk with him, listen, and share her story. When she left, she didn't think much of it, but the boy's mom came and found her.

"I don't know what you did," the boy's mom said, her face beaming, "but my kid is so encouraged—he has life again!"

Finally, after months of not knowing, a concrete diagnosis came: Devic's syndrome—a rare variant of multiple sclerosis. Ro-Ro would always have the disease in one form or another. Medicines could slow its progress and help her lead a mostly normal life. But the one thing she had been best at would be taken away from her.

Ro-Ro's basketball days were gone forever.

The concrete diagnosis brought more exact care and a quicker recovery. Ro-Ro could wiggle her toes soon, then move her hands. The family remembers this huge sense of excitement. Doctors even were shouting, cheering. Physical therapy started. That summer, after nearly a year in the hospital, Ro-Ro came home for good. By her birthday in October, she was walking again some days. By Christmas, she said good-bye to her wheelchair for good.

Ro-Ro had missed an entire year of school. She went back and graduated in 2005. Today she is almost completely recovered. She still has some pain in her lower back. Occasionally she has swelling in her spine. But the prognosis looks good. Sparrow Clubs sponsored Ro-Ro the year she was sick. A huge jazz concert was held as a benefit. The money raised helped pay off hospital bills.

This fall, Ro-Ro will begin college to become a nurse. She volunteers at the hospital, talking with patients, encouraging them as she can.

Hopefully the year Ro-Ro got sick is all in the past, Gary says. But strangely enough, he says, "I wouldn't change it for anything, as hard as it was. It was worth it to see the good that's come from it. We're on track, all of us, and closer than we've ever been."

SPARROWS OF INSPIRATION

I'm just really happy to be able

to help someone in need

and be able to give instead of get.

—SPARROW CLUB MEMBER, JUNIOR HIGH AGE

ALEXANN'S LAST BIRTHDAY

As national development director for Sparrow Clubs, CJ McPhail has met a lot of sick kids over the years. One story sticks in his memory most vividly. Soon after CJ started his job, he met Alexann Krumm.

Alexann and CJ shared the same birthday—May 31. CJ was twenty-eight when they met; Alexann was seven. A first-grade student at Central Point Elementary School in Medford, Oregon, Alexann was diagnosed with Ewing's sarcoma—an aggressive type of bone cancer that can cause tumors to grow on a person's skeletal structure. The disease often packs a double blow—not only can it disfigure, but the tumors can produce pressure on nerves and skin that causes excruciating pain.

CJ remembers the first time he drove to the house where Alexann lived. He wasn't sure what he'd find. Some kids are shy at first, particularly if they don't look like other kids. But Alexann hobbled out to meet him, grinning broadly, her butterfly henna tattoo bobbing brightly on her bald head.

A tall, thin girl, Alexann had recently undergone surgery, and one leg had been amputated below the knee. Doctors had reattached Alexann's foot to the stump to aid in prosthetic attachment. Alexann could still move the foot and impishly waved hello with it as a child would normally wave with her hand. Alexann laughed deeply, throatily, ironically—the first of many wonderful laughs she and CJ would share. Alexann had dealt with setbacks before. Even a bald head and missing leg couldn't get her down.

"Right away we had this instant bond," CJ said. "Maybe it was the same birthday thing. I don't know. It was easy to make a connection with her. She made it easy."

CJ worked with the family for several months, arranging a Sparrow Club for Alexann at her school, securing business sponsors, and handling paperwork. He visited the family frequently. Alexann was in an upswing, and her prognosis looked good. Alexann's school was all set to hold an assembly to introduce her as its Sparrow child.

But one day CJ got a phone call from Alexann's mom. Alexann's condition had taken an unexpected nosedive. She was in the hospital and the prognosis was poor.

WHO YOU REMEMBER ALWAYS

Doctors told the parents first. They had their tears privately. Then Alexann's mom knelt by her daughter's hospital bedside and filled her in. The child had a right to know, reasoned her mother. In about three months, Alexann was going to die.

Alexann was mad. She cried through her anger. She wasn't afraid, but she had wanted to beat that *stupid* cancer so bad.

Over the next few weeks, Alexann's condition worsened. As the disease slowly shattered her body, she became difficult to look at, CJ said. A softball-sized tumor protruded from one side of her head. Her skin turned colors from all the medicine—purples, yellows, dark red around her eyes.

At first, Alexann kept her spirits up. She dressed up in shawls and played in the pediatric ward, twirling and dancing like any little girl.

Soon Alexann only had the energy to lie in bed and watch DVDs. Her favorites were *Blue's Clues* and *SpongeBob SquarePants*. The Make-A-Wish Foundation bought Alexann her very own TV and DVD player, complete with a box of DVDs. She sparkled with delight.

Toward the end, it took too much energy for Alexann to even open her eyelids. CJ visited every day, sometimes twice a day. That was the hardest time, CJ said. "Alexann made little noises like muffled moans. I think she was trying to protect us. I'm sure if she had been alone she would have been screaming."

ONE LAST PUSH FORWARD

Weeks progressed, and Alexann lived on borrowed time. Doctors were puzzled—they couldn't understand what was still keeping this little girl alive.

Her mom had a theory.

It was near the end of May. Her daughter was no dummy. Alexann wanted to get presents and have fun, like any little kid. Alexann wanted to celebrate, one ultimate push forward, one final festivity—Alexann wanted one last birthday party.

Her official birthday was still several days off, but doctors were positive she wasn't going to reach the actual day. Nursing staff decided to move the clock forward. No one would need to know. They collected all the fanfare and gathered outside her room with kazoos, whistles, birthday cake, and presents wondering if they, the grownups, could keep it together once inside. CJ was with them. He didn't know either where his strength would come from, but he knew Alexann deserved the best birthday party any hospital could throw.

And they opened the door.

"We forgot all about ourselves," CJ said. "We partied. We all partied. Alexann partied best of all."

That May 31, Alexann would have turned eight. Thirty hours after her last birthday party, Alexann died.

WHEN SOMEONE CHANGES YOU

One family member didn't attend Alexann's last birthday party—Alexann's little sister. Some time earlier, Alexann had told her mom that her little sister was not allowed to come to the hospital anymore. Her mom complied. Alexann, with understanding beyond her years, didn't want her little sister to be frightened. She didn't want to leave her sister with the memory of how she last looked.

CJ went to the memorial service. Sarah, a young girl with leukemia whom Alexann had met in the hospital, acted as unofficial greeter. Sarah shook hands with everybody as they filed into the church. When people cried, Sarah gave hugs, comforting person after person—the last act of a good friend.

"Anyone Alexann's life touched was moved," CJ said. "Not just moved to tears, but moved to action. It was amazing to see what she accomplished in people's lives, even after she died."

Alexann passed away before her school could adopt her fully as a Sparrow. But that didn't stop the school. They knew the family still needed support and encouragement, perhaps now more than ever. Alexann was sponsored as a Sparrow posthumously. A car raffle was held to raise money for the family's medical bills. In fourteen days, the elementary school students raised $16,000—an amazing feat for a small school in a small town. The raffled car, a tricked-out Acura, was painted Alexann's favorite color in her honor—candy apple red. CJ went to the assembly where Alexann's best friend plucked out the winning ticket.

"It was the strangest celebration at an elementary school I've ever seen," CJ said. "They all understood they had accomplished something great, but they also understood they had lost a friend. The whole school cried at the same time. We all did."

This May 31, CJ will turn thirty-three. He's worked for Sparrow Clubs for close to five years now. He's met a lot of sick children over the years, and each is special, each loved. But one encounter sticks in his memory most vividly. CJ holds it as insight, as backup, as drive to keep moving forward no matter what hurdles life presents. It was the day a tall seven-year-old met him with a grin, balanced on one leg, her butterfly tattoo golden in the sun. CJ would know his new friend for only nine months, but his life would be changed forever.

OUR FOREVER SPARROW

I t was a Monday.

Walls and floors gleamed glossy and bright at Sky View Middle School. But for nine-year education veteran Jennifer Anderson, the brand-new school was in direct contrast to how she felt inside.

Another staff meeting, she thought and shuddered. *I just don't know how I can take one more.*

It felt like a Monday indeed—a whole year of Mondays. Staff from five and students from three middle schools had been pulled together to create the new school. Detachment, divisions, animosity, and awkwardness had characterized its first year. A common theme at staff meetings was, "Well, at my old school, this was how we did it…"

Jennifer—"Mrs. A♥" as she was known at Sky View—was a science teacher and worked with two other teachers to facilitate a leadership group. She felt disheartened by the educational culture around her. Being a teacher just felt tougher and tougher as the years went by. Generally kids seemed cynical and selfish. They seemed not to value their education. Mrs. A♥ wasn't even sure if she wanted to be a teacher anymore. To top it off, she was struggling with her marriage. Things didn't look very bright at all.

That Monday the news broke at school that Rachelle was sick. Rachelle was a great kid. Once someone dropped a bunch of pencils in the hallway. Others kicked the pencils even farther, but Rachelle stopped and helped pick them up.

"Hey guys," she said to whoever could hear her, "let's help out."

It was no news that Rachelle had been missing some school lately. No one knew exactly why. That Monday, Rachelle's friends talked to Mrs. A♥ before class started.

"Rachelle has cancer," said a close friend. She was in tears. "How can we do something to help?"

By the end of the day, Mrs. A♥ had heard the same news from a dozen students. Some were Rachelle's friends; others simply knew of her or had a class with Rachelle. Funny how many lives this winsome girl's life had already touched.

One friend in particular wanted to help. This young lady was a straight-A student, a people-pleasing seventh grader. But the prestige came with a price—an anxiety disorder that made it nearly impossible for her to handle the school's crowded hallways. She loved school, but it was just too overwhelming. She didn't want to stay at home. Teachers and a counselor worked with her in hopes that she could come each morning and try to stay a bit longer each day.

Mrs. A♥ wanted to do something—for Rachelle, for the student who struggled in the halls, for all her students. She wanted to help her students through this difficult season. Maybe the leadership class could do something. But what? Another teacher had heard something about Sparrow Clubs USA. That Monday, Mrs. A♥ phoned the club. After explaining how the club works, a representative asked if he could come to the school the next day.

"It was incredible—" Mrs. A♥ said—"to have someone come that quickly. Monday, I heard the news. Tuesday, Sparrow Clubs came and talked with us. By Friday that week, we held our first assembly for Rachelle. Now that's taking action."

Rachelle came to the assembly with her parents and sat with her peers in the bleachers of the gym. Mrs. A♥ had the microphone down on the floor. She explained how Sparrow Clubs works, then challenged the 750 students with one statement:

"If you can do one hour of community service for Rachelle this weekend, will you please stand up?"

Immediately, 750 middle school students stood. The gym rumbled with the weight of the movement. Bleachers creaked. Then students cheered. They broke loose and hollered. The whole school was standing together—standing for Rachelle—standing for what they knew could be accomplished if they joined as one.

TRANSFORMED SCHOOL

Rallying around Rachelle became the silver lining at the new middle school. Students and staff jumped in. Rachelle needed a series of experimental treatments that, to the best of Mrs. A♥'s memory, cost $1,000 every ten days. Students came up with numerous creative ways to cover that cost week after week.

Rachelle had played basketball. (Her teammates called her

"Rocky" because of her strong determination to make the most of her time.) Her team hosted a school-wide garage sale. They secured advertising and arranged for horse trailers to sit in the school parking lot to house the merchandise. That event alone raised several thousand dollars.

A coin drive was held. Boxes and plastic bags filled Mrs. A♥'s office. Kids stopped her in the hallways and emptied their pockets. She began coming to school earlier to avoid the rush. One morning a student yelled from down the hallway:

"Mrs. A♥ —Hey, wait!"

The student, towing a five-year-old girl with her, shouted "This is my little sister. She's got something for you!"

Mrs. A♥ waited for the girls to catch up. "Hi, little sister," she said. The five-year-old carried a plastic bag. Change jangled inside.

"My toof fairy came last night," said the little girl, and handed over the plastic bag. "This is for Rachelle."

Staff meetings took on a new tone. Now there were updates, freshness. Rallying around a common cause had washed the irritants away. Staff meetings were now storytelling times where teachers bragged about what the kids were doing throughout the school. The Sparrow Club eventually raised more than $40,000.

Mrs. A♥ also noticed a change in the student with high anxiety. Lately the pressure-stricken girl had been able to stay to the end of each school day.

"What's helping you do this?" Mrs. A♥ asked her.

She looked away. "Well, you always make the Sparrow Club

announcements at the end of each day. If I'm not here, I don't know what's going on with Rachelle and how to help out. I'm choosing to have courage and stay."

TO HAVE COURAGE AND STAY

Not all went well for Mrs. A♥.

She and her husband later separated.

And not all went well for Rachelle.

Despite all the good intentions and effort, not every Sparrow story has a happy ending. The following November, Rachelle lost her battle with cancer. She passed on a Friday evening. That Monday morning, school officials brought in grief counselors for the school. They knew the blow would be huge for the students who had fought so hard for their friend. Dozens of kids filled the library for days, talking, sharing, and pouring out their hearts.

Kids made a memorial to Rachelle outside the school gym—the same gym where they had all stood to their feet and vowed that they would walk with her together. A slate marker displays the dates of Rachelle's life and these words:

IN LOVING MEMORY OF

OUR FOREVER SPARROW—RACHELLE D. CALLANTINE

"ONE WHO UNITED US ALL"

Rachelle's parents placed birdhouses nearby so real-life sparrows would come to the memorial too. Flowers and figurines can be seen to this day—six years later.

When Rachelle died, students and staff weren't sure if they ever wanted to have a Sparrow Club again. It was tough to go on.

But that Christmas they made a decision. They decided the best way to honor Rachelle was to celebrate what she brought to them. They decided, together, to sponsor another Sparrow—in honor of Rachelle.

In the new year, the students sponsored Sam, a young boy with a disfiguring bone growth. Sam lived several hours from the school and was never able to visit, but the students poured out their love on Sam and his family just the same. Sponsoring Sam helped the students, Mrs. A♥ said. It helped them say good-bye to Rachelle. It helped them say hello to healing. The school has sponsored a Sparrow every year since.

At the end of that year, Mrs. A♥ looked for some students who could help spread the word to other schools about Sparrow Clubs. She needed students who felt comfortable with public speaking. The student who had personally struggled with anxiety volunteered. She spoke at several schools, and one thing led to another. The student who once couldn't stay an entire day at school eventually spoke at a leadership conference—her courage hammered out on the anvil of selflessness. Ashley went on to graduate with honors.

"Every kid has amazing gifts," Mrs. A♥ says, "and when they have a purpose, they can choose to use their gifts. We just need to invite kids to use their virtues—kids will rise to the occasion and do heroic things."

Mrs. A♥ later made a decision in her own life too.

"Several years later, I found myself in the middle of a separation from my husband," she said. "After finding my wings again as a teacher through Sparrow Clubs, I was still struggling with my personal life. I made a choice to fight for my marriage. I chose to call on my virtue and to honor my marriage vows. Here I was, surrounded in this culture of courage and determination with Sparrow Clubs staff and students. If so many kids could choose to call on their virtue to overcome difficult situations, then so could I."

A year and a half ago on a lawn at Black Butte Ranch, overlooking mountains and a pond, a pastor "remarried" Jennifer Anderson and her husband. Today, their marriage is stronger than ever.

Mrs. A♥ has renewed her commitment to education too. Today she helps educators use Sparrow Clubs as a curriculum for character building and leadership skills in public schools.

"Impacting kids is an honor," she says. "I want to do this forever. The kids, through Sparrow Clubs and school, touch my life and make my heart sing every day. I know I have been blessed to be a part of a very special thing."

TOGETHER

Laurie Crossman has worked in education for twenty-five years.
She knows what works. Currently she's the resource room
teacher/learning specialist at West Tualatin View Elementary
School near Portland. This is her story.

We have a young Hispanic boy at our school named Jesus.
He's totally blind and uses a cane to get around. Jesus is
in fifth grade now—he's been with us since first grade, so most of the
older students know him but not many of the younger ones do.

I first heard about the Sparrow program from a principal at
another school. We joined up with the other school to sponsor Jesus
together. The first thing we did was host a kickoff assembly with a
slide show at both schools. Then, throughout the year, students did
a variety of service projects. Some read to younger students; some
dug weeds in a wetlands area; others helped their grandparents at
home. One of our goals was to raise the money to get Jesus a laptop
computer that reads Braille.

During the project, I noticed some subtle but important
changes in our school. You start out thinking it's going to be all
about taking care of a student with needs, but the process really

focuses on what others can do. For instance, one student wrote that he did chores all the time, but for the first time he realized that others could benefit from what he regularly did.

Jesus was great too. He's very funny, very smart. He wanted to participate in the service projects too. So he went around to other classes and read in Braille to younger students. His favorite book is Dr. Seuss's *I Can Read with My Eyes Shut.* The irony wasn't missed on him. He read it to kindergarten, first grade, and second grade and then read some more advanced books to older students. Kids would ask him questions when he was done: "What is it like to be blind?" "What is it like to read in Braille?" "What are your biggest challenges?" Things like that.

After that, Jesus didn't seem so unusual to other students. They knew him. When they saw him around the hallways with his cane, they'd say hello and ask him how he was doing. I saw Jesus's confidence level soar too. You could tell he was happy to be able to interact with students more.

Our school draws from a mix of affluent and impoverished families. One of the good things about Sparrow Clubs is that this was something every kid could do—it really leveled the playing field and didn't exclude anybody. Everyone saw how simple it is to take care of others.

SUCCESS

Sometimes you hear about someone who is living a success story. When you ask that person what her greatest challenge is, you don't hear any venting or spewing. You hear about thriving. Sure, there are challenges, but challenges are being met. The place this person is at is a good, sustainable place.

Michelle Tisdel fits that profile. She's a coadvisor to the Sparrow program at Seven Peaks School in central Oregon. She became involved with the clubs initially as a way to spend more time with her two kids when her oldest began middle school. Her daughter talked about the difficulties she faced in this new environment. Kids could be so mean sometimes. As Michelle walked the hallways, she knew what her daughter was talking about. She thought, *Boy, if anyone needs to learn compassion, it's middle school kids.* Michelle liked the direction of the organization and the principles Sparrow Clubs taught.

"It just spoke to me," she said.

Working with the "healthy" kids, Michelle began to notice some trends. She remembers the letters her club kids wrote to their Sparrows. Note after note would encourage them to "stay strong" and to "keep going." One eighth grade girl, after meeting a five-year-old with cancer, came to Michelle with a new understanding of fairness. "I thought my life stunk," the girl said, "but I realize now how self-ish I've been."

One of Michelle's favorite stories involves a note written from the parents of a young girl named Willow. Willow had wondered what to ask for at Christmastime. Then she decided what she wanted most of all: some money she could pass along to her Sparrow child. Her parents' note, accompanied by $150, read:

Dear Willow,

Christmases will come and go,

but this one will last forever.

Love, Dad and Mom

Stories like those keep Michelle going strong. "If kids learn early the importance of community service and giving back, what a better world we'll have," Michelle says.

Michelle has been a volunteer for six years. She recruits other moms to help. She's already signed on to be an advisor for next year.

"So many people benefit from Sparrow Clubs," Michelle says. "It makes our hearts feel so good. The Clubs need to be everywhere."

THE GOLD BUCKLE

Ask Mike Sharkey how much experience he had with cows when he first volunteered at the Luke Mezich Memorial Team Roping competition, and he just grins.

"Well, I ate beef," he said.

Each year for the past four years, Mike has spent Father's Day weekend as a volunteer at the rodeo, herding cattle from pens to chutes for the various events. He works as much as fifteen hours daily, all weekend long—partial shade in mornings, full sun in afternoons.

"It's hot, dusty work," Mike said, "and you smell like a pig by the end. It makes for some very long days. People tell me I'm crazy. But I tell them I'm here to pay homage to my boy."

A FATHER'S TAKE

It's been six years since Mike Sharkey's son Dameon passed away. There isn't a day goes by that Mike doesn't remember his boy.

"If you had to go into a gun battle," Mike said, "he's the guy you'd want by your side. He was extremely loyal. He always cared about the guy next to him."

Every winter, Mike and Dameon gathered wood together.

They'd hunt around and find slash piles, picking up firewood for the winter ahead. Mike remembers his son always staying out there until the job was done, even in rain.

"He was as big as a house and as strong as an ox," Mike said. "He'd pick up a tree stump and say, 'Is this big enough for you, Dad?'"

Once, they were moving topsoil to put in a new backyard. It was a complete transformation—lawn, trees, granite sculptures, and twenty-six cubic yards of dirt. For days the duo pushed loads of dirt around, often up ramps. One day, toward the end, Mike was exhausted. He simply ran out of gas.

"I can't go on," he told his son. "I'm sorry."

"That's okay, Dad," Dameon said. "I'll finish up."

And he did.

Mike remembers his son as compassionate. Once they were walking down the hall together at Dameon's school. Dameon noticed a kid in a wheelchair sitting by a classroom door, waiting for the class to begin. Nobody was talking to him, Mike said, but Dameon did.

"He tried to brighten the kid up," Mike said. "He just went up to him and talked. He was always trying to do that, no matter who it was. I was so impressed."

What would Mike like people to know about his son's life?

Once Mike noticed that the family's grocery bills were much higher than usual. He did some investigating. Dameon had a habit of making friends with anybody. He'd invite them over, just to hang out. The Sharkey household had become a refuge for many of

Dameon's friends. Every morning, a group of them gathered for breakfast. Dameon would whip up pancakes and cereal, orange juice and muffins. Dameon didn't care how many came. What mattered was that they were cared for.

"Dameon had some pretty interesting friends," Mike said. "He didn't have any prejudice. He just took his friends for what they were."

Two of those friends—guys known for their toughness—rowed out on Lake Washington after Dameon died. They placed a wreath on the water for their friend, a tribute of flowers for someone who cared.

It continues to amaze Mike just how many people Dameon's short life touched—and in such unexpected ways. Dameon always loved tools. As a young adult he worked as a cabinetmaker. While many kids his age hang out in bars or at beaches, Dameon loved to hang out in the hardware section of Sears. A few months after Dameon died, Mike and his wife, Barb, were in Sears, and the tool lady asked how their son was.

Mike filled her in.

The tool lady wept.

The tool lady. Dameon was a friend to everybody he met.

TWO THINGS

There are two things that Mike says few people knew about Dameon. The first is that he had a great sense of humor. Dameon was a quieter kid, so sometimes it didn't show. After Dameon had received so much press for spearheading Sparrow Clubs, a human-interest story ran about him in one of the major tabloids.

"It was actually a beautiful story," Mike said, "even though it was a tabloid. When Dameon saw it, he just laughed. He said, 'My goodness. I'm between the Wonderbra ad and the two-headed bear.'"

The other is this—much more serious, more impacting.

When Mike was younger, he used to drink heavily. Wine was his favorite—as much as three bottles a day every Thursday through Sunday (he made sure he never came to work drunk). It was a self-destructive track. The drinking would have killed him for sure, he said. His son noticed, grew concerned, and took action.

"One day Dameon looked at me and said, 'Dad, don't you dare die and leave me alone on this godforsaken earth,'" Mike said. "That's what he said—word for word." Dameon was about fourteen years old. "I'll never forget it. I quit drinking the next day."

How important were his son's words to him?

"Dameon saved my life," Mike said. "Absolutely—my son saved my life."

HAPPY FATHER'S DAY

Two years ago, the rodeo instituted a new award—a gold buckle given in Dameon's name for outstanding volunteerism. The awards ceremony comes at the end of the weekend, sometimes late at night.

The first year, Mike won the award.

"It was kinda embarrassing," Mike said. "It was a surprise to me. I went on stage and got my award. When my wife and I were driving back to the motel, she looked at the award. She turned to me and said, 'Happy Father's Day.'"

And when Mike tells that story today, he cries.

Sparrows of Selflessness

It feels so good to know that I am making a difference in someone's life. It's so easy to be concerned with only yourself in high school, and it's nice to do something good for someone else.

—Sparrow Club Member, High School Age

MILES FOR MILES

At 10:00 p.m., a nearly full moon shone on Crater Lake in the midst of southern Oregon. It was June, but snowdrifts, luminescent in the late spring thaw, still covered the sides of the road. Forty-year-old Scott Stemple laced up his running shoes and began to run. His destination: the parking lot at the Ruch School, a tiny K–8 near Jacksonville, Oregon—one hundred miles away. It would take twenty-four hours of running to reach his destination—a solid night and day of pounding, blisters, spitting, and sweat—that is, if all went according to plan. Scott had run marathons before—26 miles, 385 yards. He had even done a 50-kilometer race once (about 31 miles) but never a distance this great. This was nearly four marathons back to back. Any number of things could go wrong.

The first four miles were spectacular. No cars were out. The mountains looked so close that Scott thought he could almost reach out and touch them. He ran down the middle of Highway 62, a red strobe light strapped to his back for protection, head lamp illuminating the road before him. Woodland animals chattered and guffawed, cheering him on. This was more than a run. It was a mission.

Scott, a seventh and eighth grade teacher at the Ruch School, was raising money for Miles Johnson, a first grader with a cardiac condition. The school had adopted Miles as their Sparrow. Kids held car washes and various fund-raisers. Scott wanted to do something more. Scott had dubbed the run "Miles for Miles." He wanted to raise attention for the boy; he also wanted his community to become involved. He knew the run wasn't just about Miles Johnson—it wasn't about just one kid. It was about *any one kid,* about people getting up off their couches and reaching out.

Scott knew firsthand what it was like to sit on a couch. More than six years earlier—December 31, 1999, to be precise—he was lying on the couch watching the Ducks play Minnesota in the Sun Bowl, and he rolled over.

"It was like my stomach rolled over five seconds behind me," Scott said. "Three little words changed my life. I said to myself: *Dude, you're fat.*"

That New Year's he made a resolution. He had never been much of a runner, but he bought a baggy jogging suit—size 38. His first run was at night because he didn't want people to see him. He puffed and huffed about a mile and then went home. The next night he went out again. Six years later, he still has that old jogging suit. He wears it around the house every once in a while, partially as a joke to bug his wife, Kara, and their two kids, partially as a reminder of the shape he used to be in. He's lost forty-five pounds and is down to a size 30 waist now. Today he runs fifty to sixty miles per week.

Scott made another change in his life after beginning to run. He had worked as a businessman, intent on winning the rat race. But he quit his job and went back to university. He wanted to be a teacher—someone who could make a difference in kids' lives. And not just any teacher—he wanted to teach middle school students, a purposeful move to affect kids at one of the most challenging and insecure times in their lives.

"Kids in junior high can be extraordinarily misunderstood," Scott said. "Yes, they can be aloof, crazy, madly inconsistent. But they also have an exceptional capacity to care—to do the right thing. They just need the right opportunity."

Scott's new mission: to teach kids *how to truly live*.

MISSION: POSSIBLE

Scott ran through the night into dawn. Coming out of the mountains proved tougher on Scott's body than he had planned. Runners typically alternate between running up and down hills—the change lets their legs use different muscles. But this run had been all downhill so far, murder on Scott's upper thighs. He felt tight and cold; he was beginning to hurt much earlier than he'd expected. He was also behind schedule. Friends and students joined him on various legs of the run—some for four or five miles, some for longer. Still, Scott had a long way to go.

As the sun began to heat up the day, Scott switched on his iPod. His headphones blasted a hard-driving mix of rock 'n' roll bands like Everclear, Green Day, and Alice in Chains. In the early morning, he came into Union Creek, a small wedge in the middle of the road known as the best berry-pie stop in southern Oregon. A Guns N'

Roses song came on, something Scott had listened to in his younger days.

"Take me down to the paradise city,
Where the grass is green and the girls are pretty.
*Oh, won't you please take me home."**

Paradise city. Stopping at Union Creek sounded like paradise to Scott, but he kept going.

The day grew hot between Shady Cove and Medford—just a long straight stretch with lots of traffic. Mile after mile rolled on. Scott grew tired, the pie shop long behind him. Worn. Dusty. Cars zipped by him anonymously. His quads were killing him. His mileage meter showed mile fifty-five—more than halfway through, but still so far to go.

Then a funny thing began to happen. That morning one of the area newspapers had a front-page story on Scott and the run. The picture, taken at an interview a few days earlier, showed Scott with Miles on his shoulders. People had read the story that morning, and they started to stop.

The first car honked and someone handed Scott a check. Another slowed and the driver made a donation. People waved. People cheered. Three little girls each gave one dollar out of their piggy banks. By the time Scott ran into Medford at about mile seventy-seven, people on the streets knew he was going for gold.

In Medford, Scott stopped at several elementary schools, as planned. Schools all over the town were cheering him by now.

---

* Lyrics excerpt from Guns N' Roses, "Paradise City," *Appetite for Destruction.*
Copyright © 1988 Guns N' Roses.

He felt good; his pulse rate was low; he didn't feel tired at all. His legs simply ached. At the final school in Medford, Scott met with a television crew. The interview was supposed to take two or three minutes—a sustainable rest for a warm runner. Instead the interview took more than ten minutes, and it proved incredibly hard to stand for that long. When Scott started running again, his legs felt trapped. It was like a cement vise was clamped around them, tightening its grip with every stride. Scott had twenty-three miles to go—almost one full marathon.

He ran for five more miles until he got to Hoover Elementary School—the second-to-last planned stop before the end. The last three-quarters of a mile to Hoover were excruciatingly painful, Scott said. Now it was like jagged shards of glass were imbedded in his legs. Every time he stepped down, the shards cracked. By then Scott had run for a solid twenty hours and forty-five minutes. When he reached Hoover, he collapsed on the grass.

Kara met him at the stop. She began to massage his legs. It was past 7:00 p.m. A group of well-wishers was waiting for him at the final destination, still eighteen miles to go. Even if Scott averaged a respectable ten-minute pace, he still had three hours to the finish, not including one more stop at another school. Miles Johnson was waiting at the end with his mother. The students in Scott's classroom were there. They would wait as long as it took, Kara said, but still, there was something Scott needed to consider.

"I know you can make it," Kara said. "I know if it was left up to you, you'd go on. But this run has never been about *you*. You've done what you set out to accomplish. Now it's time to shut it down."

Scott looked at his wife and nodded his head. He lay on the grass a few more minutes, his legs in unbearable pain. He hobbled over to the car. After running for eighty-two miles, Scott took one last look at the road and got in.

THOSE WHO RUN WITH YOU

Trent, a seventh grader in Scott's classroom, had vowed he would run the final twelve miles with Scott. Twelve miles is a good hurdle for a young man. Scott wasn't sure if Trent was up for the challenge, but Trent insisted. "Look, if you can run a hundred miles, I can at least do twelve," Trent had told him earlier. Trent wanted to make the run so badly.

When Scott pulled up in the car at Oak Grove Elementary—the last stop before the end—Trent met him at the car door.

"Dude," Scott said, "I'm sorry. I'm really sorry."

A lot of seventh graders would have given you attitude at that point, Scott said later. But Trent had tears in his eyes. He came over and gave his teacher a hug.

"Mr. Stemple, don't worry about it," Trent said. "You did great."

Scott spoke briefly to the rest of the teachers and students, then got back in the car. The crowd cheered as he drove on down Highway 238.

But Scott wasn't convinced. As he sat in the car he began to feel sorry for himself, he said, almost pouting. He didn't feel like he had finished. He felt like he had let everyone down.

Others disagreed.

About a half mile before the Ruch School, Scott's final stop, sits a corner store. As they neared the corner, Scott and Kara began to notice a sea of colors. Faces and signs became visible. About 150 kids, parents, and teachers waited at the store. The Ruch School only has about 190 students total. Many in the crowd wore "Miles for Miles" T-shirts. The sea of well-wishers came running up to the car, some jumping up and down, all cheering—they just wanted to get close. Scott climbed out of the car and joined the group.

This last half mile they would travel together.

Together, they set off for the school, walking, running, skipping, dancing—a swirling mass of color and joy. About a third of the town's population met the group at the school. Scott shuffled his way to the finish line and walked across. The crowd roared. The race had never been about him. It was always about something much greater. While Scott went to ice his legs, the party continued with food, banners, posters, a group playing Capture the Flag. Five boys had shaved their heads, and each had painted a letter on his chest to spell out M I L E S. It was just one unbridled celebration of happiness, caring, togetherness, and community.

Then Miles Johnson's family drove up. It had gotten too late for the little boy, and he had gone home to rest. But now the party was in full force. Miles jumped in to celebrate with his town.

"What is it about Miles?" Scott wonders today. "Miles is a wonderful kid, but we did this because a little boy and his family needed help. It could have been for anyone—anyone who needed help. We would have done this. This was about compassion and community. We accomplished our goal."

A Gift to the Family

It's not easy to make a living as a professional photographer. It's like being an artist or a singer. Everyone wants to take pictures. But Kevin Kubota had made it. He and his wife, Claire, had formed Kubota Photo Design; they had years in business together. Kevin was best known for his work at weddings and for portraits: happy occasions. He traveled around the country doing seminars and teaching photography techniques. It was a successful life, and everything seemed right on track.

But one day, he got an invitation to do something more.

A friend who worked for Sparrow Clubs contacted Kevin and asked him to take some pictures of Sparrow kids for a fund-raiser. The pictures would be enlarged and used as posters at the event. Kevin had taken pictures for charitable organizations before but was hesitant at first about volunteering for Sparrow, even a bit choked up. He imagined it would be very hard to photograph sick children. Their situations seemed so desperate. He hated photographing anything depressing. But he agreed to volunteer his services anyway.

What was he getting himself into?

The Good You Never Knew Could Exist

On his first shoot, Kevin met a family with two young girls, both with medical difficulties. The younger girl, about four or five, had just lost her hair due to chemo, but she had the cutest face, just the greatest smile. Her older sister, about six or seven, was so sweet with her, Kevin remembers. The older sister hugged the younger sister, following her around, so caring, so attentive.

Kevin and Claire set up the shoot in the backyard. Their aim is always to photograph kids in whatever situation feels most comfortable for the children. The sisters played on their junglegym. Kevin crouched down to their level and started taking pictures. Mom was close at hand. You could tell she was carrying more of the weight of the medical situation, Kevin said, but the little girls didn't seem bothered at all. (A photograph taken during this shoot is used on the cover of this book.)

After the shoot, Kevin packed up and sat in his car and cried. He didn't feel sorry for the kids. He felt sorry for getting upset about the trivial things in life.

"It just put things into perspective for me," Kevin said. "Here were these kids living with a desperate situation, but they were so positive, so living in the moment. It wasn't a depressing experience at all. It was the opposite of that—it was uplifting."

Kevin was hooked. He volunteered for more. His pictures were featured in Sparrow brochures, fliers, and on the Web site. Some went to newspaper articles about Sparrow children. Others were used at auctions and fund-raising events. Today he's taken pictures of about twenty-five Sparrows. He puts as much priority and effort into his volunteer shoots as into any paying job.

In addition to the inspiration he's received, one of the best parts of volunteering is the gift Kevin's pictures provide. Families with sick children are almost always faced with large medical bills. Having a professional photograph taken is seldom a priority. Families are often very appreciative of the pictures, Kevin said. And in the hard times, when a child doesn't make it, a photograph is often one of the last best memories.

One year, the school where Kevin's son was in first grade sponsored a Sparrow, a little girl named Hannah, who was in the same class. Kevin took pictures of her at home in her family's living room. Hannah was fighting cancer and had no hair. Kevin took pictures of her running around the room, comfortable, playing, hamming it up for the camera. Hannah passed away later that year. Her parents said the pictures Kevin took are some of their most cherished keepsakes.

But not all the photo sessions are easy.

One little girl, about two or three, was partially paralyzed. Her head flopped, and she couldn't focus very well. There weren't a lot of choices of locations to take pictures. The little girl lay on a couch and got hold of her favorite book. She peeked over the book and gave a big smile. *Click*. That was the shot.

Kevin still teaches seminars around the country. He encourages photographers to volunteer their time and services as well. Others have followed suit. Stories come back of similar success.

JUST DO WHAT YOU CAN DO

One of the best parts of photographing any Sparrow child, Kevin said, is getting connected. Kevin's philosophy of taking pictures is to lay down any pretense and get rid of any barriers.

"It looks pretty silly sometimes," Kevin said. "I get down on the floor and play with kids, chat about what they're doing, make them feel comfortable in their world."

One little boy's photo shoot came right around Christmas. Kevin got down on the floor with him by the tree and played with train sets and cars, taking pictures as they played. When Kevin got ready to leave, the little boy wasn't finished yet. He ran back to his bedroom and grabbed more toys.

"I like that other boy," the child said, pointing at Kevin. "He's fun to play with!"

A connection can also be hard to make. For one shoot, Kevin drove ninety minutes in a blizzard. A teenage mom was living with some friends in a run-down neighborhood. Her daughter, about two, was paralyzed. The father had taken off. It was a bleak situation, Kevin said.

"The child was just lying on the couch—it was hard to get her to smile, hard to get any reaction at all," Kevin said. "The mom was calm, very nice. She eventually held the child on her lap, and we got some good shots, but I felt so helpless. It was like, 'What will become of them?' There wasn't a whole lot anybody could do."

How does Kevin resolve times like that within himself?

"My purpose in taking pictures for Sparrow is to have people look at them and be inspired to get involved," Kevin said. "I want to move people to action. Everyone has something they're able to give. Get involved. How powerful it is in your own life to give back and help others."

A PLACE TO FEEL RIGHT

Think San Francisco, California.

Think the massive arch of the Golden Gate Bridge, the regal white columns of the Presidio, the ballparks, the Bay, the attitude and outlook of a major cosmopolitan region.

Now think Bend, Oregon.

Think pine needles, tumbleweeds, and a population of about seventy thousand.

Bend has its own beauty, its own pull and attitude, but for Emma Liliedahl-Allen, a move from San Francisco to Bend with two months left of eighth grade seemed like relocating to Jupiter.

"I found the transition really hard," Emma said. "I didn't feel profiled or anything, but I didn't grow up here, I didn't know anyone, and then there's this extra *thing*." With a black father and white mother, Emma, although fair-skinned, is clearly biracial.

A school counselor suggested that Emma get involved in something to meet new friends. On the third day of her freshman year in high school, Emma saw a wall sign advertising Sparrow Clubs. She had never heard of Sparrow before and had no idea what the club was about but decided to check it out. The club could have been anything for all she knew.

"I'm convinced something led me there," Emma said. "It was more than me just aimlessly walking around."

Emma had volunteered with the Camp Fire organization since first grade and was no stranger to community service. The Sparrow Club at her new school had just begun. It didn't feel very cohesive at first, Emma said, but the direction it was going felt familiar. She jumped in. She met people. She made friends. The club grew. The rest of her school became involved. Her new community became involved. Things were looking up.

At the start of her tenth grade year, Emma signed up again. One problem—it was just her and a bunch of twelfth graders. Emma knew if she didn't act fast, the club would disintegrate when all the seniors graduated at the end of that year. So she became president.

"I began to feel a real ownership of it my sophomore year," Emma said. "I felt a commitment to the club beyond anything else." She led the club all that year, then again her eleventh grade year, and finally her senior year. Today the club is a vibrant, solid part of the school she just graduated from.

When asked to pick a favorite story from over the years, Emma says it's as impossible as a parent trying to pick a favorite child. But one stays with her most closely. Emma had always baby-sat. She did well at her job and always took it seriously, so something about the club's Sparrow child her sophomore year hit close to home.

That year the club sponsored a baby named Maggie, a victim of shaken baby syndrome at the hands of her baby-sitter. Emma cried when she heard Maggie's story. One night the parents went out. Their child was perfectly healthy. When the parents came back home, their child was in a coma.

"That will always stick with me," Emma said. "Because I'm a baby-sitter, it was a huge reminder what an important job that is. Parents are leaving a life with you. You need to take such responsibility for that."

When Sparrow Club members first met Maggie, the little girl needed to wear a helmet. The left side of her body was paralyzed. She couldn't walk. The club organized fund-raisers and special events throughout the year for the child they sponsored.

And throughout the year, Maggie made progress. Amazing progress. By the end of the school year, Maggie still needed a helmet, but she had learned to walk again. She could even run. The club was ecstatic to be able to play a role in her recovery.

Emma renewed her fund-raising efforts. She helped organize a tongue-in-cheek male beauty pageant for her school. Word got out, and guys started to take the event seriously. Guys took it as a challenge of their bravado—a chance to win bragging rights in their school. The event raised $7,000 its first year, $11,000 its second, and $21,000 its third. The event moved beyond just a school fund-raiser to include the town's involvement.

"Twenty-one thousand dollars is a lot, but it's just a small amount compared to some of the medical expenses families have to pay," Emma said. "I know we can do more."

Spreading the Light

As Emma graduates, she passes the reins to a new Sparrow Club president. But the lessons she's learned will stay with her forever. In addition to meeting her initial goal of simply making some friends and fitting into a new community, Emma says the club has helped shape her outlook on the future.

"Changing the world is possible," Emma says. "There is light at the end of the tunnel, and I hope to help spread the light. Not just by myself, but as part of a community."

Emma plans to attend Minnesota's Macalester College in the fall, possibly pursuing international communications. Her dream job, she says with a grin, is to be a personal shopper while she's in her midtwenties, but she also knows that ultimately "that's not a job for a grownup." She'd like to start her own nonprofit organization some-day to help people—somehow, someway. She doesn't know how exactly, but she knows that's the direction she wants to head.

Has it all been worth it?

"Absolutely," Emma says. "It's funny, you know. You don't letter in Sparrow Clubs, you don't get scholarships, but ten or twenty years from now, you'll still have this memory of helping somebody in need. I really take that to heart. To me, it's more important. There's no other way to do that except through service to others."

What Parents Give

When a child is sick, what does it require of parents? Much? Most? All? Parents often say that whether to give is not the question. When they become parents, the question is already answered. All. Everything. Always. When a child becomes sick, the thought is simply: *Whatever it takes to get our child healthy.*

Still, there comes a time when parents are faced not with whether they will give all, but whether they *are able* to give all. That can be most difficult, for when the answer is no, frustration must turn to faith. And when the answer is yes, love must become a degree of action seldom experienced before then.

A Rare Blow

Carrie Kuba had a difficult pregnancy. The placenta ruptured, and Isabella (Bella for short) was born four weeks premature by C-section. Bella was placed in the neonatal intensive care unit (NICU).

Everything looked okay at first, after the rocky arrival. But within a few days, doctors noticed too much protein in Bella's urine. Bella was diagnosed with congenital nephrotic syndrome, a rare kidney disorder that affects only about one in forty thousand children worldwide.

Her prognosis looked bleak. Many cases of the syndrome are fatal within the first year. Some are controlled with early and aggressive treatment, including early kidney transplantation. Carrie and her husband, Martin, went into vigilant mode. This was a serious disease that needed urgent medical management. Treating it would be difficult, with a high risk of complications. What would happen to their precious new baby?

By "coincidence" (the Kubas say it was no coincidence at all), the doctor at the hospital in the Kubas' small town had studied the syndrome in Finland and was familiar with it. He recommended transferring Bella to a larger hospital. A friend in the Bay Area knew a doctor who was part of the children's nephrology team at Stanford's Lucile Packard Children's Hospital, one of the best university hospitals in the nation. Wheels began to turn at once. Within a week, Carrie and Bella were airlifted to Stanford and received the last bed available in the NICU.

With the syndrome, a person's kidneys can't hold protein, so the body has no protein, which it needs to grow and thrive. At Stanford, a catheter was inserted into Bella's chest to give her protein infusions. Carrie and Martin needed to learn to work the pump (it took three twelve-hour days of intensive training), for they were to give Bella the infusions each night from 9:00 p.m. to 3:00 a.m. while she slept.

A ten-month treatment program began, with regular flights back and forth to Stanford. Bella did well for the first six months, but as she got bigger, the protein wasn't enough, and she became sicker.

Once when the family went in for a regular checkup in the winter of Bella's first year, the doctor took one look at Bella, went white as a sheet, and said, "Bella is in 'failure to thrive' mode. We have to take her kidneys out within the next seventy-two hours. Plan to be here for the next two to three months." Both of Bella's kidneys were removed, and she was put on dialysis. Carrie and Martin had wanted to prevent this, but Bella was simply not gaining enough weight. In a medical irony, her kidneys needed to be taken out so she could get stronger and grow.

The goal became to get Bella big enough for a kidney transplant. For four months, Bella was at home. Martin describes this as one of the most difficult times. The parents manned the dialysis machine, which ran all night long. Bella had a little tube into her perineum that would pump fluid in and filter her blood. They didn't have to watch the machine the whole time, but neither parent ever got much sleep. Because the dialysis filled Bella up with fluid, it stretched her belly to the point that it was very painful, and this went on all night. Martin works as a software engineer. His employer proved flexible, often allowing him to work outside the office.

And Bella grew. The question now was, could a match be found for the transplant? And if a match was found, would the person donate?

WHEN YOU GIVE

With kidney transplants, close relatives are tested first to be a match. Martin and Carrie were both tested. Martin was deemed the best match.

The scenario was laid out for Martin: It would mean massive

surgery for him. He would need to be in the hospital for almost a week. Recovery would take at least six weeks after that. He wouldn't be able to walk for a while. Any movement at all would be difficult at first. For the rest of his life, he'd have to be more careful—high blood pressure and diabetes would pose a greater risk for him. Martin had never had any type of surgery before.

Would the father donate a kidney to his daughter?

"It was never even a question," Martin said. "When we found out I could be a donor, it was good news. Of course, I was a bit afraid…"

Father and daughter were prepped for surgery at the same time. Bella's surgery began at 7:00 a.m. and continued into the night. Martin's took less time but was still as risky. And for Carrie during this time? What is it like for a wife to have both her husband and her daughter in the hospital and in surgery at the same time? Martin believes it was in many ways harder than what he went through. It meant Carrie bore the weight of the situation by herself.

Both surgeries were considered successful. Recovery proved harder for Bella. Part of her lung collapsed, and she had difficulty breathing. She had to start taking antirejection medication right away, and it always takes a while to get the dosage correct. Bella was released from the hospital after three weeks. For a month after that, she came to the hospital every day for tests.

When Martin recovered, he flew home to work. Bella and Carrie had to remain near Stanford for four months, with Martin commuting every chance he could get. Fortunately, Carrie's parents live twenty minutes from the hospital and always had a room ready for the family, however long they needed to stay. Martin has good medical insurance, but everything still added up. Air Life bills, deductibles, prescriptions, travel costs, food...Bella also needed an expensive blood-pressure machine and respite care.

Bend High School students in the Kubas' hometown sponsored Bella through their school's Sparrow Club. They did fund-raisers and sent cards and Christmas presents.

"It was very special for us," Martin said. "The gifts were wonderful, but it was the emotional support that was best. Just knowing we weren't alone."

When a Community Stands with You

Martin and Carrie had lived in their hometown for one year when Bella became sick, having transferred from another state for a job. Carrie is American; Martin is originally from the Czech Republic. He had immigrated to the United States about nine years before.

"We were both amazed at how people came and supported us financially and emotionally during this time," Martin said. "People we didn't know made things easier for us in a difficult time. It is so important to have a good community."

Today, life is slowly getting easier. The transplant has been considered a success. The disease is in remission. Bella's a bit behind for her age in height and weight, but she's catching up fast. She has a feeding tube that goes in through her nose to her stomach because the new kidney needs more hydration and she can't drink as much as she needs. She's still hooked up to a feeding pump at night. Bella will battle complications for the rest of her life: Her immunity is lower, and she'll always be at risk for rejection of the donated kidney. Stanford remains involved in all medical decisions. She will need a new kidney when she is in her thirties.

Overall, Bella is doing well. She loves to dance and twirl in circles. Bella's a social kid who loves to be around other kids. She has a Siberian husky named Dakota that she loves to play with. A favorite father-daughter activity is playing outside with a ball. Carrie and Martin read to Bella a lot, another favorite activity. Each night Bella takes her books down from a shelf, sits on a lap, and flips through the pages.

When a favorite book about a farm comes up, Bella always asks Martin to do all the animal sounds—*ba baaa-baaa* goes the sheep, *cock-a-doodle-do* says the rooster, *moooo-moooo* goes the cow...

And, grateful for this good moment, Martin does.

SPARROWS OF DIRECTION

Helping our Sparrow is something that is hard to put into words. For me, it is being able to put my faith into action. I know that I am helping do something that makes a difference in this world.

—SPARROW CLUB MEMBER, HIGH SCHOOL AGE

THE LONE STEER

There are two hard questions that everyone associated with Sparrow Clubs must wrestle with daily:

What does it feel like to be a parent with a sick child?

What does it feel like to be a parent of a child who died?

For Sparrow Clubs USA board president Steve Mezich, the questions hit close to home. A thirty-nine-year education veteran, Steve currently works as principal at St. Catherine's private school in north Seattle, where he's also coadvisor to the school's Sparrow Club. Steve plans to retire soon—it's getting harder for him to keep up with kindergarteners. When he does retire, he plans to devote even more time to volunteering with Sparrow Clubs.

"There's a lot more to do," Steve said. "Sparrow is an amazing program. I challenge anyone to show me a curriculum that can influence the hearts and minds of kids like Sparrow can."

Steve Mezich has been with Sparrow from its inception. Years ago, he worked as principal at Kamiakin Junior High School, where Jeff Leeland was a teacher and athletic director. Steve witnessed firsthand how Jeff's son became sick, how bills became insurmountable, and how one young boy named Dameon Sharkey stepped forward with $60, the mustard seed–sized beginnings of what has become a national organization today. Steve saw a whopping $227,000 raised in just four weeks—more than enough to cover Jeff's son's medical care. Steve and Jeff's question from the beginning of Sparrow Clubs was this: If an outpouring of empathy, fund-raising, care, and action can happen at this school, why can't this happen all over the country? Steve was a board member from the start.

Steve believed in the club. He believed in what the club could do. But a tragedy in his own family would further steel his resolve to help families in need.

When Life Stops

Two of Steve and his wife, Jan's, four children had grown up loving horses. Steve was a hobby team roper, and Lisa and Luke both rode in junior rodeo associations around Washington State. It was a special part of their lives.

Luke competed at an amateur level. His specialty was calf roping. Like most rodeo events, calf roping is not for the faint of heart. In this event, a 250-pound calf is released from a chute and scurries across an arena. A cowboy on horseback rides after it, swirling a lasso. The cowboy must rope the calf, jump off his horse, pick the calf up, and secure three legs. Professionals can do it under ten seconds. At age sixteen, Luke could do it in a highly respectable twelve—good enough to win the state championship.

"It was a pretty cool deal," Steve said. "Luke was a superb calf roper. He was fast and consistent. That's what it takes."

At six feet tall, Luke was a good-natured kid who always had a smile for everybody. He played baseball and basketball and made friends easily. He graduated and got an apartment. At age twenty-two, his future looked bright. One morning Luke phoned his dad. His car was in the shop that morning and he needed a ride to work—could Dad take him? Steve drove his son to work and picked him up at the end of the day. They ate dinner, then Steve took Luke back to his apartment.

"I looked him in the eye and told him I loved him," Steve said. "He did the same. It was a strong, solid moment."

For some reason, Steve felt compelled to watch his son walk into the apartment. Steve sat in his car for a few minutes afterward, just thinking. Luke faced challenges like any kid did, but Steve had always encouraged him to have courage, do what needed to be done, to get up and keep going.

Steve started his car up and drove home. It was a moment he held close.

Late that night, Steve and Jan heard a knock on their front door. It was the type of unknown knock that brings a sense of terror only parents feel. A sheriff stood at the door. His eyes looked down.

"Mr. Mezich," the sheriff said, "there's been a fatal traffic accident tonight involving a young man named Luke Mezich. We're wondering if he's a relative of yours."

Steve remembers a sense of panic, dread, confusion, and pain, but also a strange confidence. It was their worst nightmare come true, but God would get them through this, somehow, someway.

"Yes," Steve said. "He's my son."

When You Go On

The next few days were a blur. The Meziches notified family and friends, made plans, cried and grieved. The house was full of people. Every note, every card, every comforting touch—each bit of support meant something special, something unique.

Luke's memorial service was packed. In the church's foyer, the Meziches placed one of Luke's trophy saddles from a few years back, a pair of his boots, and one of his cowboy hats.

"We knew the only way we would survive was to turn to God," Steve said. "We looked to Him for understanding, healing, and courage. From that moment, we simply chose to go forward."

Crowds dwindled. Friends and family stayed close, but real life picks up again after a while. The Meziches coped the best they could. Steve returned to his teaching, but days were hard. Weeks were hard. Years were hard. How do you ever deal with losing a child?

In Washington State, educators are encouraged to retire after a set number of years. After a certain point, educators actually *lose* benefits if they keep teaching. Steve reached that point and retired from the public school system. But he still felt like a young man in many ways. He applied to be principal at a private school.

Steve remembers the moment well. When he drove to the interview, he felt a strange nervousness. Luke's death still hung in his thoughts. Could Steve summon the strength to truly keep going forward? He sat in the parking lot at the school. He felt trapped by his own doubts. Unable to move.

"It was the strangest thing," Steve said. "Sitting in my car, I could actually feel Luke's hand on the back of my neck, just the same way I used to put my hand on his. It was like he was encouraging me to do what needed to be done, to get up and keep going, to have courage and move forward. I got out of my car, went in for the interview, and came out as principal of St. Catherine's."

THE TRIBUTES IN OUR LIVES

That spring, Steve and Jan made a decision. They wanted to do more. They wanted to do something that would memorialize Luke and do something emotionally and spiritually good for the family. They chose to give back.

That summer, over Father's Day weekend, they held the first ever Luke Mezich Memorial Team Roping competition. The event was a benefit for Sparrow Clubs—to raise money and also to spread the word about what the clubs did. The first competition was held in Woodinville. Cowboys and cowgirls came from all over. The event grew. Soon it was moved to a bigger venue, in the Ellensburg rodeo arena.

Ten years later, the event is still going strong. There's calf roping, team roping, barrel racing, events for kids, and more—one long weekend of horses, dust, action, prizes, and rodeo fun. It's become a huge celebration of life for families all across the Pacific Northwest. Last year the event drew 1,187 teams. The Meziches' daughter, Lisa, and her husband, Will Schmidt, organize the weekend. The

Meziches' grandson, three-year-old Brayden Luke Schmidt—named in honor of his uncle—helps lead horses to the arena.

Steve and Jan can't believe it every year when they start to see the first pickup trucks and horse trailers drive into rodeo fairgrounds for another year's event. That next day at 9:00 a.m. comes one of the best parts of the weekend for them.

After all the fans and competitors are called together and welcomed, Steve thanks everyone for coming in Luke's memory. He calls people to look forward to what Sparrow Clubs and the spirit of compassion is doing today. There's a moment of silence, and then in Luke's honor a lone steer is released from a pen. The steer runs the length of the arena—a tribute to Steve and Jan's boy, who loved the outdoors so much. The crowd is silent. Then another steer is released. This time in honor of Dameon Sharkey—the young boy who started Sparrow Clubs. Both tributes to the past. Both tributes to the future.

"It's our way of saying thanks," Steve said. "Thanks for all the support received. Thanks for all the support people continue to give."

I Found What I
Was Looking For

I 'm not the type of person who just jumps into something right away," says Julie Lowes, mother of two. "But I was looking, searching. I needed to do something beyond myself."

A dental hygienist, Julie speaks with the type of reserved efficiency of one who researches something first, then does it very thoroughly, very well, very completely. Job done.

"I had been feeling for quite a while that I needed something deeper," she says. "I led a busy life, but was looking for a place to be involved in the community where I could serve others."

When Julie's son, Dylan, now thirteen, was in elementary school, Sparrow Clubs was offered as part of the curriculum. Julie remembers attending her first Sparrow assembly along with her son. It brought her to tears.

"It's all very moving," she says. "You can't *not* want to help."

Julie helped out in the Sparrow program at her son's school at first. She liked the structure of the club. What impressed her was that the kids weren't just doing fund-raisers. Sparrow Clubs was a creative way for kids to make a difference. About a year later, Julie jumped in.

"I decided to make some changes in my own life," she says. "I wanted to do something meaningful."

Her daughter, Gabby, now a junior in high school, was just starting middle school at the time, and Julie and a friend helped start a Sparrow Club there. The club was initially held during lunch hour. Julie remembers the first time the group of middle schoolers walked into the room. Only a handful came—her daughter and a few of her friends mostly. Even then the group was squirmy. They had a million ideas all at once and wanted to talk about them all— getting organized and underway would be the first challenge. Julie realized she would need to be firm, take the reins, and get down to business.

Slowly the group grew, both in size and in responsibility. As club advisor, Julie soon realized she was leading the group in no small task. These kids would need to help organize the rest of their school in leading service activities—the kids would need to make announcements, speak at assemblies, work on projects, and encourage other kids to help. This was Leadership 101–type stuff. Julie was teaching her group highly important life skills.

"Teaching kids how to give back is huge," Julie says. "Sparrow Clubs helps them think outside themselves. When they see others in need and know they can do something to help, they realize life isn't all about *me, me, me*."

When You Go Forward

The club grew. Julie completed the first year and tackled another, then another, then another. She recruited her husband, Peter, who heads a regional business called Lowes Commercial Properties, to become a business sponsor. He helped organize a triathlon. Julie also recruited her employer, Bend Family Dentistry, to take part in a Christmas giving program. There were hot dog sales, car washes, cleanup days, bake sales, and more.

It was about the kids, always the kids.

Julie remembers when Brooke, a six-year-old in remission from cancer, came and visited her group. Brooke's head was bald, her face swollen from chemo and steroids. The club kids asked her questions: What was her favorite animal? What kinds of hobbies did she like?

With the quiet wisdom of one much older than her years, Brooke described to the group what life was like with no hair. When she went bald, her dad shaved his head too.

Something in her expression caught the group off guard—a poignant portrait of the love of a father for his little girl. These kids knew all about it. Some were secure in it. Some longed for it. When Julie looked around, the group was sobbing.

"I'll never forget that moment," Julie says.

That was spring. In the summer, Brooke died. Julie went to her memorial service.

"This is what I do," Julie says. "I found what I was looking for."

TOGETHER WE WILL SOAR

Dana Jackson helped start a Sparrow Club as a high school sophomore. She is now a university student, intent upon becoming a pediatrician. This is her voice.

As I walked past the undersized white box, my eyes shifted to the side. It was too early, too heartbreaking, too real, too small.

Before me, beside the coffin, Stephanie's mother screamed and fell to her knees. Stephanie's father bit his lower lip, trying to stop the tears. How recently joy and laughter had filled their house because of their young daughter's life.

It was all too much for me to take in.

WHAT GOOD IS A SOUP GREEN CAR?

Only a few months earlier, Stephanie's mother had discovered a lump in her child. A cancerous tumor had wrapped around Stephanie's colon. Surgery was impossible due to the tumor's location and Stephanie's age. Chemotherapy was the only option. Since

Stephanie's condition was serious, her mother was forced to stop working. Her dad often had to miss work to drive them to a hospital located three and a half hours away. Stephanie's family was new to America from Mexico and did not speak any English.

Stephanie entered my life when I was a sophomore in high school. As president of the Honor Society, I wanted to start a club that everybody could join, regardless of their grades, popularity, or athletic ability. My desire to unite my school through the hearts and sentiments of my peers led me to Sparrow Clubs USA, where everyone's common interest appeared to be a love for children, helping others, and compassion. In our club, we had athletes, artists, chess players, and school leaders. It became a popular club—everyone who was anyone was in Sparrow Clubs.

When Stephanie's family was introduced to our club, we immediately fell in love with the little girl. She had brown eyes and curly brown hair and was so shy that she held on tight to the back of her mother's knee, barely peeking from behind. The woman who brought the family to our school explained Stephanie's condition. She appeared so healthy—it was hard to imagine that her little body was slowly being killed by the cancer.

After we met Stephanie and her family, club members pressed to help. As high school students, we found it difficult to understand that death comes for "invincible" young people. Death even takes those too young to understand it. For several months, we helped Stephanie's family any way we could. Everyone wanted to volunteer. People in the community couldn't believe what was happening. Our school was challenging the stereotype that high school students are lazy, selfish, and only concerned with material things. We surprised others by asking what we could do for *them* and not what they could do for *us*.

I saw the hearts and minds of my peers grow and change after weeks and months of service and volunteering. We began to understand the power of working together to impact Stephanie and our community. Businesses and newspapers commented on the difference we made, and we gained more support. This was a tremendous help because we received more money and items of better quality for the family.

On Stephanie's good days, I'd drive over to her house and play with her. I'd take all the supplies we had collected during the week in my '77 Buick Century. Kids would laugh at my car because it's pea soup green and huge, but I could pack it floor to ceiling with stuff for Stephanie's family. When I say I packed it, I mean trunk, backseat, back window area, floors—even the front passenger seat was piled as high as possible.

I'll never forget the first time I pulled up to Stephanie's house with a load of supplies. Throughout high school I had been embarrassed to drive up to anyone's house or anywhere around town. Everybody else had brand-new cute cars. But for the first time in my life, when I pulled up to their house, I was proud of my car, proud of who I was, and proud of all those behind this wonderful cause. I was blessed with this large car not only for my transportation but also to transport fulfillment of the needs and dreams of others.

As I got out of the car to unload I glanced up to the front door and saw Stephanie resting in her mother's arms. Her mother seemed to be using the door frame to keep her balance. Tears ran down her face—tears of disbelief, triumph, and faith. Her eyes said "God bless," and she started to pray out loud in Spanish. "Thank You, Lord, for blessing me with not only my daughter, Stephanie, but for all these children acting as angels..." Her voice faded and I could no longer hear.

THANK YOU FOR MY DREAM

After unloading all the groceries and toys, I played with Stephanie. As a child, I had spent a few years living in the Dominican Republic and Honduras, and I understood how scary not knowing the culture and language around you can be. During my childhood, I'd learned enough Spanish to be able to communicate with Stephanie's family.

Around that time, I began to think a lot about what I wanted to study someday in college. I'd always dreamed of becoming a pediatrician. When I was younger, on the playground at recess, I always wanted to help others who fell and got hurt. My little sister had often been the unwitting patient of my young doctor dreams. She sat through checkups where I would fix her up with Band-Aids, listen to her heart rate, and check for a fever. But as I grew older, my confidence and my aspirations of becoming a pediatrician lessened. I felt less sure of myself and the person I wanted to become.

At Stephanie's funeral, I knew with certainty I would become a pediatrician. The helplessness I felt over her death overwhelmed me. I wondered if I could've saved her if I were a doctor. I might not have been able to, but I would have liked the chance to help more than I did.

Coffins should not be made so small, and young children should not die. I want to become a doctor so I can save children like Stephanie when it's God's will. When it's not His will, I can at least decrease a child's pain and suffering so he or she can live as happily as possible.

Sparrow Clubs (and Stephanie) helped me find my calling and my confidence in who I am. Every time I consider giving up my dream because it's too hard, I think about these children and how they smile despite their hurt and misery. They even manage to make others smile. Children like Stephanie teach us the meaning of strength and inspiration. Sparrow Clubs helps me remember that life is about those we touch, and more importantly, those who touch us in ways that inspire us to be better people. It is through these experiences and helping others that we can learn to embody the life God desires.

My experience with Stephanie lit my fire. She is the reason why I currently attend one of the nation's top schools for premedicine, where I'm majoring in both Spanish and English. I also plan to study abroad to enhance my Spanish skills. After I graduate from medical school, I want to run an affordable, if not free, pediatric clinic in Central America where I can help children. This may be possible with United States sponsors and donations to help me with my crusade to save sick children. It is these children's faces that will allow me to pass on Stephanie's spirit and inspiration through my life work.

Dedicated to the memory of Stephanie Sanchez-Romero: May your spirit dance and laugh in heaven forever... I'll see you again one day, and there...there we will become sisters in heaven.

THE GIFT

Rob Bonner teaches eighth grade science and leadership class at Crook County Middle School. There are sixty-two students in the leadership class, in charge of dances, assemblies, and the overall climate of the school. As part of their curriculum, the school ran a Sparrow Club this past year. This is Rob's story.

This is my second year as leadership advisor, but it's the first year we've done Sparrow Clubs. As far as I'm concerned, there won't be another year that we don't do it. When all is said and done, we're hearing it said throughout our school that this was an amazing year.

Our Sparrow was Katie Morris, an eleven-year-old with an inoperable brain tumor. Doctors gave her a 20 percent chance of survival. She needed forty-two chemo and thirty-three radiation treatments over seven weeks to buy her more time. Katie was enrolled in our school for a while, and she has an older sister at the school in eighth grade.

At the beginning of the year we held an assembly and showed the Sparrow video. The amount of caring was just enormous. The vouchers for community service started coming back immediately.

Students satisfied the requirements for hours, then just kept going. Brooks Resources was our sponsor. Then Les Schwab Tires became involved. We had checks for $1,000 coming in at one point. The school board asked us to give a presentation. It grew pretty big.

One of our coolest fund-raisers was a pyramid thing where a bunch of people shaved their heads if a certain amount of money was raised. The more money in, the more people shaved. Students, staff, teachers, the principal, the vice principal—even one female teacher, Michelle Jonas—shaved their heads. About six female students also shaved their heads because of Katie. In the end, we raised about $5,000.

Katie visited several times during the year. Her situation remains terminal, yes, but she's having lots of experiences. She recently took her whole softball team to a Mariners game. She's amazing. I'd say she brought the whole school together.

One way she brought the school together was through tears—the people who cried surprised you, the kids you think are too tough to show emotion. It's really powerful. I've been in education for nine years, and this is proof that kids can be unselfish, caring. It's the power of people rallying together. That's the true gift.

THREE YEARS OF SPARROW

Natalie Weber was a Sparrow Club member for three years during high school. She recently graduated and is heading for university, where she hopes to start a Sparrow Club. Her intended major at university is "something in the medical field" with the aim of helping people. This is Natalie's story.

When I started high school, my life revolved around school and golf. I played varsity golf as a freshman, and our team won the state championship that year. Grades were hugely important—I was a straight-A student. Basically I felt invincible, like nothing bad could ever happen to me.

My friend Stefanie was involved with Sparrow Clubs our freshman year. They had a party for club members at the end of the year. She wanted me to go, but I didn't because I didn't feel like I was part of it. In the fall, our sophomore year, we saw a poster on the wall for Sparrow Clubs. Stefanie said we had to go, so we did.

I was glad I went. I loved Sparrow Clubs from the start. That first year we sponsored a boy, about a year older than me and from another school. He had been in a car accident and was in a coma. I was really caught off guard—getting hurt could happen to someone my age. The boy survived, he came out of his coma, and we met him toward the end of the year when he talked to our club about his experiences. He expressed thankfulness to us. It felt really good—that we had actually helped this guy and his family. For me it finally clicked. More important than being a good daughter, good sister, good student, good golfer was helping other people.

Helping people became my number one passion. I wanted to get even more involved. At the end of my sophomore year, our advisor, Mrs. Currie, asked me if I wanted to run for president of the club. I had to give a speech and wasn't comfortable with public speaking. But I gave it anyway, and I was president my junior and senior years.

Being club president was a completely new experience compared with being a member. At the start of my junior year, we needed to raise membership, so I talked to a number of different groups of kids at school to try to get them to come to our meetings. At the first meeting in September, all the desks were full and people were lined up in the back of the room! It was the most members we'd ever had attend a meeting.

We organized a lot of quality projects that year, including a pumpkin patch festival, working at an ice-cream parlor for a night and having all tips and half the proceeds go to our Sparrow, putting together mailings for an area hospice organization, tutoring students at a nearby elementary school, and more.

Another major job of being president was sitting on the student advisory board for all Sparrow Clubs in our region. The board was made up of two reps from each of the area high schools. We'd meet to bounce ideas off one another. The most crucial purpose was planning the annual regional "Find Your Wings" talent show. Planning the show was an extremely difficult but rewarding task. An advisor helped with the sponsorship and budget, but the rest was up to us. We held individual school talent shows to pick three acts to advance to the regional show. We recruited volunteers to run the sound system, lights, backstage, curtains, and such. We put up posters and went on local morning shows as advertisement. We even asked local talent scouts and influential people in the community to be judges. The experience of coordinating all this helped me mature into a member of my community rather than just some student with a limited voice.

The Sparrow child we adopted my senior year touched my life perhaps the most. Autumn was three and had tumors in her stomach and kidneys. Early that year she'd had both kidneys removed. In December, she and her family came to school for our annual holiday assembly. The Sparrow Club and teen-parent program had gathered about thirty to forty presents for her. I will never forget the look on Autumn's face when all the presents were piled around her on stage. She melted every heart in the auditorium that day.

The middle of January was Autumn's fourth birthday. The vice president of our club, Julie Doolin, and I drove to Autumn's aunt's house for the party. Even with both kidneys removed and a feeding tube, Autumn ran around with her cousins like a typical tough four-year-old. Then her aunt, Chessica, made a toast to Julie and me and the entire club for all our support. I was not expecting this. It was so generous for them just to invite us to their family gathering, and now they were honoring us!

A few months later, we received some heartbreaking news. Autumn's condition had taken a drastic turn. The tumors had multiplied too quickly, and the doctors couldn't do anything to help. They estimated she had three months left. I found out via e-mail one day after school. It was like all the air left my body. All I could do was stare blankly at the screen as tears rolled down my cheeks. I couldn't comprehend how a beautiful, vibrant, fun-loving four-year-old could go through all that.

The next few days we had officers meetings to talk about the shock and to decide what we could do for her and the family. One of the officers wrote a beautiful poem about what knowing Autumn had meant to her. We made it into a card and had all the members sign it. We also took pictures from the holiday assembly and pasted them in. A week later the officers took the card to Autumn's aunt's house. The strength Chessica possessed was amazing. As we gave her the card, you could tell how touched she was, and I knew at that moment there was nothing more we as a club could do—it was up to a higher power.

Thanks to Autumn, I have learned to appreciate every single moment I have free of pain and with my family.

Right now she and her dad are in Portland, making her last weeks peaceful and loving.

Being in Sparrow Club and hearing heartbreaking stories and

miracle events has made my life more whole than I ever thought it would be at eighteen. I have met so many inspirational people that I will keep in contact with years down the road. I am just so thankful that I was part of this great organization. Anything I can do to pass on the message and the feelings I have, I will do.

Sparrows of Purpose

It has showed me that I can help.

I can make a difference in the world.

—Sparrow Club Member, Junior High Age

A Legacy Continues

I t all started with some golf clubs.

The brand of clubs, the style of clubs—it doesn't matter now. What Barb Sharkey remembers is that her son Dameon wanted some. He had saved hard—$60 so far—not bad for an eleven-year-old kid.

So the call at Barb's work one afternoon surprised her.

"Mom, can we go to the bank after school? Please," Dameon said from the school pay phone. "I want to take my money out of savings."

Barb was reluctant when she heard her son's plan. People are proud. It can be tough for anyone—even someone in need—to receive a gift. But Dameon persisted. In fact, he *insisted*. So Barb phoned Jeff Leeland—a teacher at Dameon's school and the intended recipient of the money—to talk the matter over with him. Jeff's son Michael had leukemia and needed a bone marrow transplant.

"Dameon doesn't need to do that," Jeff said. "Please, just tell him to be there for us. That's enough."

"Well…" Barb said. "Dameon's not taking no for an answer."

ONE BOY WHO CARED

Dameon was a really private kid, Barb says. He didn't do things for glory. After the media got hold of the story, things snowballed. Something inspired people about Dameon's donation. Money kept coming in and coming in. In four weeks, twelve $5 bills had multiplied into $227,000—more than enough for Jeff's son to have the procedure he needed.

The attention on Dameon intensified, but he took it all in stride. Dameon was suddenly a hero—a sharp contrast to how the boy had felt for most of his life.

Dameon had always been a big kid. He weighed twelve pounds fourteen ounces when he was born. By the time he was nine he weighed 150 pounds. When Dameon was in elementary school, someone phoned Child Protective Services, wondering about the situation in the home. The event only frightened Dameon. From then on, he was afraid someone would take him away.

Because of his weight, Dameon was depressed a fair bit, Barb said. This caused more eating. It wasn't a good cycle. Once, in elementary school, four boys beat Dameon up and pushed him down a hill. Dameon broke the growth plate in his foot in the fall. He walked on crutches for several weeks and with a limp for the rest of his life. The experience helped make him acutely compassionate to anyone in pain.

"I'm not saying he was a saint," Barb said. "But for as young as he was, he was very wise. He always cared about people."

After Sparrow Clubs USA began, Dameon played an active roll as a volunteer. He graduated and became a cabinetmaker. He died at age twenty-one, when a cut on his leg became infected with some tainted wood resin.

"You understand it so much more when it happens to your own child," Barb said.

IT LETS OUR SON LIVE ON

Since Dameon's death, Barb and her husband, Mike, have devoted themselves to volunteering with Sparrow Clubs. Barb speaks at school assemblies, presents awards, and talks with hurting parents and family members who have sick children. The Sharkeys also help out at the Luke Mezich Memorial Team Roping competition each year.

Two years ago at the rodeo, a prize was given in Dameon's honor for outstanding volunteerism at the event. The prize is a big gold belt buckle with three garnets in it—Dameon's birthstone. On it is a picture of a child with a horse, kneeling before a cross. The first year, Jeff and Steve Mezich presented the award to Mike. Barb and Mike became presenters of the award the next year.

"Sparrow Clubs gives us a sense of fulfillment," Barb said. "It lets our son live on."

It was hard for Barb to get on stage to present the award. There are difficult memories, sure, but it was actually physically hard. Barb's health has not been good for years. Arthritis. Bone spurs.

About a year ago she had surgery to remove a tumor. Today, she has no cartilage in her knees. She gets around with the aid of a walker.

"When people don't know you or what you're going through, it can be easy to judge," Barb said. "That's always been the story. But just because you look different or don't move as easily as someone else, it doesn't mean you don't have a heart."

A Team's Inspiration

Bill Bigelow works as sports editor for the Bulletin newspaper in Bend, Oregon. This is his voice.

While I had been aware of Sparrow Clubs for a number of years, I knew little of their real potential until fall 2004.

That's when I learned of a six-year-old boy named Brendon Moore who was dying of a rare form of cancer but whose remaining days were being brightened by his involvement with the high school football team in his tiny hometown of Culver.

Through Sparrow Clubs, young Brendon—who knew he was seriously ill but not that his condition was terminal—became the adopted Sparrow child of the Culver High football team.

As sports editor of the *Bulletin* newspaper in nearby Bend, I was intrigued that a bunch of high school football players would take an interest in a child and family with this difficulty. I was skeptical that such a predicament could be comprehended by teenage boys.

Turns out I was wrong.

Brendon clearly became something special to the Culver football team. He attended the team's home games and many of its practices. The team presented Brendon with an authentic Bulldogs football jersey—number 2—which, big and baggy as it was on the frail little boy, he wore everywhere from his kindergarten class to bed.

The team's fondness for Brendon went beyond the football field. Through a number of community service projects sponsored by Sparrow Clubs, the team raised hundreds of dollars for the Moore family—enough to allow Brendon's father, Steve, to leave his construction job in order to make the most of his remaining time with his son.

Word spread about Brendon and the football team, and what had started as a Sparrow Clubs project evolved into a cause around which the Culver community and much of central Oregon rallied. A generous cattle broker from nearby Madras was so moved by Brendon's story that he paid for the Moore family to travel by plane to Southern California and spend four days at Disneyland.

In early November, an article I wrote about Brendon and the football team appeared on the front page of the Sunday *Bulletin*. In my twenty-five years as a journalist, never before had anything I'd written generated such abundant and heartfelt feedback. Clearly, Brendon Moore's story had an impact on those who learned of it.

But what I found perhaps most interesting was not how a high school football team had come together to bring joy to a dying boy's waning days. Rather, it was the impact Brendon had on a rough-and-tumble group of teens.

For my story I interviewed a number of the Culver High football players. Each one shared with me his tale of how his relationship with the team's Sparrow child had affected his life. Perhaps Brian

Stills, a senior running back and linebacker, said it best for the entire team.

"The whole thing has kind of put life in perspective for me," Stills said. "The way he [Brendon] has to fight for his life every day…it really makes you appreciate life."

What those young men told me about their humbling experience of being part of Brendon Moore's short life demonstrated to me that Sparrow Clubs serves to do more than provide help for children in medical crisis and their families. It also provides valuable life lessons for those who adopt a Sparrow child.

The Bulldogs didn't win many football games that season. But they won the heart of a dying little boy (Brendon passed away less than three months after the season ended). And in the process they became better people.

Said Kurt Davis, veteran Culver High coach, of his team's Sparrow Clubs experience: "Teenagers have this feeling of invincibility. I think an experience like this maybe makes 'em check their hole card…. Football players are supposed to be all macho and cool. I think this has been an opportunity for them to let their guard down a little and reach out with a feeling of compassion. And maybe it allows them to take a look at how fragile life can be."

What Seek Ye?

People ask Terri King, office manager for Sparrow Clubs USA, how she can work with sick children all the time.

Terri's answer: "How can I not?"

For Terri, her journey of faith began several years ago, shortly after Sparrow Clubs had been started. At the time there were two staff members on board (only one of them full time), and both worked out of the trunks of their cars.

Terri worked as a customer service manager for another company then. It was a solid job with a dependable paycheck. All told, she'd had a twenty-seven-year career in the insurance industry. Life was steady and trustworthy. The future looked good—predictably good.

But one small phrase would change everything.

With a Bible study group, Terri took a trip to Greece led by national speaker and author Beth Moore. The trip was a whirlwind from the start. The teaching sessions began immediately after a twenty-four-hour flight. Terri found herself suddenly removed from everything familiar. She saw the Acropolis, Mars Hill, Corinth, Athens—remnants of another time, tributes of another age. The Bible passage Beth spoke from begins at John 1:37. In that passage,

Jesus asks one question that hit Terri's open heart. The question stuck with her, rolling around in her mind. Terri couldn't dislodge it, nor was she sure she wanted to.

The question is this: "What seek ye?" (KJV).

What seek ye?

In other words—what do you want? Jesus was asking his followers what they were truly looking for in life. What are you truly searching after? What are you looking for? Where does your security, direction, and purpose lie?

In the passage, Jesus has a simple answer to the question He poses. He tells His followers simply, "Come and see."

COME AND SEE

What does it look like to step out in faith?

"I needed to be aware of a plan God had for my life," Terri said. "But I didn't know what that plan was. That question kept rolling around in my mind: 'What seek ye? What seek ye?' I didn't know what I was looking for. But my heart was open to something more."

When Terri returned to the States after that trip, her son Tyler, age eleven, was knee-deep in a project that resembled Sparrow Clubs. Terri watched as Tyler participated in food drives, delivered food, and made and sold "sock snowmen" as part of a fund-raiser. Tyler was enthusiastic about helping out. He had an atypical brightness about him. As a mother, Terri thought, *Something's happening here.*

A friend of Terri's helped out with accounting for Sparrow Clubs. The friend knew Sparrow needed an office manager. She forwarded Terri's name. A Sparrow representative sent Terri an e-mail.

"I didn't know much about the organization," Terri said, "but I was interested."

Terri went for an interview. When she came back, she knew that working for Sparrow was what she wanted to do. The future was unknown, but her sense of calling was clear. It was a new organization with few clear procedures in place, and Terri would need to take a salary package one-third less than what she was making. But she felt resolute.

"I just had this confirmation," Terri said. "God had it all under control, and this was something I needed to be doing."

In September 2003, Terri began working for Sparrow Clubs. She secured office space and helped put procedures together. She quickly found out that her new job was unlike anything she had experienced before. She's still a customer service rep so to speak, but working with families with sick children proved much different than the insurance business.

"My job used to be about quickness and efficiency," Terri said. "People wanted things done right away. But with Sparrow, families come into the office and often don't want to leave. Coming to the office isn't an errand to them; it's finding sanctuary. The families that come here all have hurting children. Oftentimes, the parents aren't able to get out much. I soon found out that I needed to stop and listen—and listen, and listen, and listen. It's become a real ministry."

Around the organization, Terri has been deemed "the office

crier." A box of tissues is always on her desk. These are never "cases" or "numbers" she works with, but real people going through really hard times. Terri feels honored to share in their experiences.

As part of her job, Terri reads every service voucher written by school kids who participate in Sparrow projects. The vouchers are handwritten accounts of what each project has meant to each kid involved. Terri has read thousands of vouchers over the years.

"Again and again I see an awakening in youth," Terri says. "They see that they can do something that matters."

A SAFE PLACE

Terri's new role has also been an invitation to miracles.

A few years back, Sparrow Clubs was helping out a little girl, Maggie, the victim of shaken baby syndrome. When the crime initially happened, Maggie was taken by helicopter to a hospital in another city. Maggie's parents were told their daughter wouldn't live through the night. Unable to accept that prognosis, they prayed, "God, we know that's what the doctors are saying, but we know You can do something else."

Over the next several months and years, the same little girl who was once so near death stopped having seizures, started talking again, and eventually made an almost full recovery. To this day, doctors have no medical explanation. Terri just smiles.

Another time this same little girl needed to have a medical procedure done at a clinic near the Sparrow offices. Maggie fought the sedative, flailing around so much that her mother took her out of the doctor's office. She brought the child over to Sparrow. The girl had been there before; it was a familiar environment. Terri sat with the mom and Maggie in the Sparrow offices, speaking to the child in hushed, soothing tones. The child eventually calmed and fell asleep. Her mom was able to take her back to the doctor to have the procedure.

There are hugely hard moments too. Terri has attended several funerals over the years. One, for a little boy named Tyler, sticks with her always. Tyler had been a Sparrow at a nearby elementary school. Students had sold friendship bracelets as a fund-raiser for him. Almost all the kids wore one. When Tyler's memorial service was over, the students pinned their bracelets to a large poster as they filed out the door of the gym. The poster was shaped like a big red heart and said, "We love you, Tyler."

"It was such a tribute," Terri says. "Kids expressed so well what a friend Tyler had been to them."

"What Seek Ye?"

For Terri King, a journey of faith started with one question. It's a phrase Terri lives by today.

"To me, it means, 'What you call me to do, Lord, I'll follow,'" Terri says, "even when you never dreamed your life would go that route. Sparrow has been such a huge blessing in my life. It's been an unexpected direction. When God calls you to step out in faith, there's blessing. Often it's not easy, often it involves self-sacrifice, but the reward is far greater than you could ever imagine."

SOMETHING INEXPLICABLE

John Churm is the co-owner of a Red Robin in central Oregon. He's the business partner responsible for operating the restaurant. This is his voice.

My involvement with Sparrow Clubs started at the suggestion of one of my partners from Medford, Bill Powell, who had been involved with Sparrow through his Red Robin there. Bill was very upbeat about what it did for kids, schools, and of course, Sparrows.

Initially, the idea of so many helping so few troubled me conceptually. Then I met Jeff Leeland (executive director of the club) and Karen Farley (area director of the club). I believe it's important that you have the courtesy to let people share about their programs or events. Our budget was full, and I really did not feel I had another penny to spend. I thought it would be just a nice courtesy visit. We get solicited by everyone! I feel bad that we can't help everyone, but I believe very strongly that it is my responsibility to help as many as possible. Most of our "marketing" funds are spent this way. We don't do much radio or television because people always want to have their

PTA event sponsored, or their run, or walk, or jump, or bike, or paddle, or…on and on and on.

We met at Red Robin. It's very seldom that I encounter someone who—how would you say it? This person is the *stuff*. It's like you know that God is here and God is in the conversation. No offense to Jeff, but he's not particularly eloquent. He's soft-spoken, nice, and generous in spirit, but that is not what drew me in. It was as if God Himself were standing behind Jeff, waving His arms, saying, "Do this as a business sponsor." I was not captivated by Jeff's message as much as an overwhelming sense that this was something we *had* to do. "Don't think about it, just do it."

We started sponsoring Sparrow Clubs four years ago. In addition to our sponsorship responsibilities, we provide meals for a Sparrow family every Friday. Our mascot shows up at assemblies. We always host an appreciation lunch for the students at the end of the club year. This is our way of thanking them for all their hard work. We also sponsor various auxiliary events that Sparrow is doing, such as the Mr. Thunder Pageant at a local high school this year. We did this through my son, Chris, who was in the pageant.

I could tell you about the personal growth I see in kids in the clubs we've sponsored. My daughter Maddy comes home excited after every club day and event. I could tell you about the hard work of the volunteer parents on the club level. I could share about the gratitude of the Sparrow parents, and the Sparrows themselves and their sparkle of hope. More than anything though, I want to express my gratitude for the opportunity it has given my business to give back to the community. Representing our three partners, Greg

Hubert, Bill Powell, and myself, it helps us be the kind of people we want to be.

Sparrow Clubs inspires kids to look beyond themselves and their own needs and give to someone who can't give back. That's what it does for us too. What happens when you do that? Many people have come up to me and thanked us for our generosity and what it means to them. Sure, this has a direct business benefit, but that's not why we do it! The kids are the stars here. They are the ones putting their hearts and care into making the program work and earning the Sparrow dollars. I don't want to take away from that.

What Sparrow has reminded us (and keeps reminding us) is that we as a business must always live outside ourselves, seeking opportunities to give to the world we touch and exist in. That is the true gift of Sparrow…to everyone.

I've owned restaurants in the past, and when I left those situations and communities, guess what? No one starved that I know of! When you strip it all down, what you're left with is a relationship you've made with the community. If you haven't tried to fill the community's bucket as much as they've filled yours, it's not a vital relationship. The relationship "bank account" gets drained or overdrawn. We must constantly be looking to make deposits, and Sparrow is a great way to do that. It helps us stay focused on this vital relationship.

An Unexpected Purpose

The Ruch School near Jacksonville, Oregon, had nearly been closed the year before. Declining enrollment prompted cutbacks in cash-strapped Oregon schools, said school officials. Something drastic needed to be done.

Community members weren't convinced that the school's doors should be boarded up. There had always been something more to the tiny community school than just the three Rs. The school reflected something of the region. It stood for something. A plan was hatched to add grades and attract more students. An agreement was reached. For one more year, the school would keep its doors open. Then another decision would need to be made.

The School with Open Doors

That year, a seven-year-old named Miles Johnson began first grade at the Ruch School. His family had moved to the area about a year earlier. Miles didn't know much about school board politics. All he and his mother, Phyllis, hoped for was that he would make it through the year still breathing, his heart still pumping strong.

Before Miles was born, Phyllis had a prenatal test to check on the baby's development. Something was wrong. Another test showed heart problems, extent unknown. Three times, medical officials asked Phyllis to consider an abortion. Three times Phyllis said no.

Miles was born a month early by C-section. He weighed eight pounds, three ounces, a big kid for arriving that early. He had his first open heart surgery at five days old. The roller coaster had begun.

Soon after the surgery, Miles caught a virus and went to the hospital. Emergency room pediatricians shrugged and sent him home to die. But one doctor knew a heart specialist and made a call. Over the next few months, Miles was in and out of the hospital. At one point, he flat-lined—clinically dead. At another, his kidneys failed. For six months he was blind, only able to see light and darkness. An infection set in, and he had a tube placed in his stomach. At eighteen months he had an open-heart bypass. A few years later, another. He had coils and shunts put in. Once, just before a family trip, his pulse rate dropped to thirty-five. Miles had a pacemaker put in.

The verdict: Somewhere along the line, Miles would need a heart transplant, probably before he's thirteen, definitely before age twenty. These days, at age seven, he tires easily. He gets blue in the lips and fingers. He needs to nap in the afternoon.

But other than that, he's one amazing kid.

One Amazing Kid

Miles has a brilliant mind. When he was only two, he put together puzzles while sitting in his highchair. Today he keeps his three older sisters on their toes—Brittany, eleven; Lexus, ten; and Chandra, nine. Miles is the organizer in the family. He loves to cook breakfast for the family. Hard-boiled eggs and cookies are his favorite.

Every morning his alarm rings at 6:00 a.m. Then he goes to wake his sisters.

"He's not bossy about it at all," Phyllis said. "He just keeps tabs on the whole household."

Miles was adopted by the Ruch School, the same school that had almost closed, as its Sparrow child. Students rallied around the little boy throughout the year. One of the teachers at the school, Scott Stemple, organized and ran a hundred-mile race in Miles's honor. Tons of people came out on race day. Newspapers and television crews picked up the story. It turned into a community celebration of compassion, caring, and joy. People saw their lives as bigger than themselves. One teacher remarked at the end of the event: "For no other reason—this was reason enough to keep the school open."

Funny how one little seven-year-old with a heart condition could affect a community to this degree.

"When Miles walks down the hall, it's like he's ten feet tall," Phyllis said. "I've always felt he's here for a reason. One of Miles's teachers once gave her class a writing assignment: 'What do you wish for?' Miles wrote: 'I want people to care about me.' He knows now that they do."

The future is still unknown for Miles Johnson. Only time will tell what unexpected purposes the little boy's life will hold for him, for his family, for his world.

A Sense of Urgency

E very Friday night during the school year, twenty-year-old Chelsea Louie, a junior at George Fox University, leads a group of college students under Portland's Burnside Bridge to deliver chicken, sandwiches, and stew to homeless people. The group, called Urban Services, also takes food to another location some forty-five minutes away.

Helping others has become a way of life for Chelsea. It doesn't matter where people live or what their needs are, Chelsea wants to help however she can.

A social work major, Chelsea is planning to spend a semester in Uganda and Rwanda volunteering with Food for the Hungry, an international relief agency. She believes people can make a difference in the world, even if it's a small difference.

For now, she's still in America. This past semester, Chelsea led a group of students to meet a family with a sick child living in an area Ronald McDonald House. The students helped clean the home and interacted with the family. Chelsea wanted the students to see how people can quickly go from financial stability to poverty because of a medical crisis.

Without a doubt, Chelsea's passion lies with helping people—both at home and around the world.

But it wasn't always like this.

WHEN YOU SEE A BIGGER WORLD

As a freshman in high school, Chelsea's world revolved around friends and sports. "I played soccer—that's pretty much what I did then," she says. She had volunteered once, but only as a way to get credit for a class.

Then during her sophomore year, her twin sister, Brittany, was diagnosed with Arnold-Chiari malformation, a structural problem affecting the cerebellum, and needed surgery. Chelsea saw her sister transform from a normally vivacious person to tired and withdrawn. Sometimes it felt like friends didn't understand. Chelsea also witnessed what it felt like for a family to be under an unexpected financial strain. Fortunately, Brittany was on the road to recovery after about a year.

When a Sparrow Club was started at a nearby youth group, Chelsea signed up right away. The club sponsored a little boy with an immune disorder. The group held car washes, raffles, and doughnut drives. At Christmas, they took presents to the family.

"Basically, I just showed up at the first meeting and said, 'I want to help in any way I can,'" Chelsea says. "I felt such a sense of urgency, maybe because it was so personal to my own story—what I had been through with my sister."

Awhile later, a Sparrow Club began at Chelsea's high school. She became more involved, helping with setting up meetings and getting friends involved. The club sponsored other children. Chelsea became vice president of the club her senior year.

"Once I got involved, the focus of my life changed," Chelsea said. "I was less focused on myself and more aware of things outside myself. It gave me a sense of responsibility."

Chelsea's life would never be the same.

Now, nearing the end of her college experience, Chelsea plans to lead a life dedicated to helping people, wherever, whenever, whomever. She credits Sparrow Clubs with the life change. After she graduates from college, she plans to work for a nonprofit organization, perhaps overseas, always helping people.

"Before Sparrow Clubs, my ideas about the future were very limited," Chelsea says. "It was always about the here and now—the moment. I believe we have a responsibility to help out in whatever capacity we can. I want to provide people with a glimmer of hope about what's important. That's what my life is about now."

Sparrows of Triumph

❧

Being able to help...has been a wonderful thing for me. I want to make a difference in the lives of people who need help, but sometimes I feel like what I can do isn't enough.

—Sparrow Club Member, High School Age

FOR KEEPS

This afternoon, when Florida resident Lisa Christman dropped off her three-year-old daughter, Lauren, at her first ballet class ever, something caught in her throat, and Lisa stayed to watch. Lauren twirled on tippy toes with the other girls, arms in a circle in the air, all decked out and foofy in their pink tutus and leotards.

Toward the end of the lesson, Lauren turned around and looked at her mom. The little girl waved, a giant smile on her face. Lisa smiled and waved back, and when her daughter was absorbed in the lesson again, turned and cried privately. Her daughter was taking ballet lessons! Lisa never believed she would see the day.

NOT IN YOUR HANDS

Everything about Lisa's pregnancy was perfect. She only gained twenty-nine pounds. Lauren was ten days overdue, but first babies often are. The child arrived a healthy eight pounds, three ounces and twenty-one inches long. Perfect. Everything just perfect.

When Lauren was ten months old, she developed a little cold. Normally, she was a "fat and happy" baby, Lisa said, but the congestion was worse than usual. Lauren also had a tiny bump on the side of her temple. Nurses said to wait a couple days—everything would clear up.

But by the evening, two days later, the bump on Lauren's head was continuing to swell. By this time, her eyes were almost swollen shut. Doctors who heard the symptoms described over the phone thought it might be an allergic reaction to penicillin. But Mom and Dad knew it was more. The Christmans called an ambulance and rushed Lauren to a children's hospital in Orlando, about an hour's drive away.

Lisa sped up the freeway in the ambulance with Lauren. Her husband, Brian, followed in the car. Lauren needed to be strapped to a gurney for the ambulance ride. The baby was crying. It was raining heavily that night, and Lisa describes the feeling as "freaking out."

"As a parent, you're in such a protective mode all the time," Lisa said. "At that moment you feel so helpless. You don't know what's happening. You're just listening to your baby crying, and she's strapped down. Your child is not in your hands anymore."

By the time the ambulance arrived at the hospital, the left side of Lauren's face was paralyzed. A hoard of specialists were called—neurosurgeons, infectious disease specialists, and much to the Christmans' horror, the police.

Because Lauren had a bump on her head, policy dictated that an investigation needed to be held. That night, while their daughter was undergoing test after test, the Christmans were taken to a small room in the hospital, interrogated by Child Protective Services, and accused of abusing their child.

"I couldn't believe it," Lisa said. "We answered question after question. Finally I just told them, 'I'm done—I'm going to go hold my daughter,' and I walked out."

The state didn't have to wait long for a medical determination. This was no bruise on the side of Lauren's head. It was a tumor. The next morning, Lauren was in surgery. The tumor had grown into her skull toward her brain. Surgeons entered behind Lauren's hairline and scraped the tumor out. Her face turned a Frankensteinish black-and-blue.

The worst was still to be discovered. Another cancer, called Burkitt's lymphoma, was raging throughout Lauren's body. It's the worst type of cancer—very rare—doubling in size every twelve hours. People have been known to die within a week of diagnosis. Lauren also had two massive tumors on her kidneys and another aggressive tumor behind her right eye, so large that it was making her eye bulge. Prognoses ran the gamut. Anything was possible: recovery, blindness, or death.

Lauren was put on steroids immediately to reduce inflammation. Lisa and Brian called doctors worldwide—Florida, the Pacific Northwest, Cincinnati, London—to figure out the best plan of treatment.

"This was a subject we knew nothing about," Lisa said. "We gathered massive amounts of information. About the only certain thing we learned was this: most people who had what our daughter had eventually died. But we stayed focused and did what we needed to do. We were on our knees every second praying."

Chemotherapy was started within two days. Lauren had another surgery to implant a catheter in her heart to administer chemo. The healing chemicals she received were so toxic that her tiny veins couldn't handle them. Nine months of chemo were mapped out. The cancer would have an atomic bomb dropped on it, but in the process Lauren's immune system would be totally destroyed.

Brian needed to return to work. Lisa set up house in the hospital. She moved into her daughter's room, sleeping with her in the same bed because she was still breastfeeding and because she was afraid that Lauren would roll over at night and pull her heart line out. Lauren spent most of her days being read to or watching The Wiggles videos. Lisa brought a red wagon to the hospital. She wanted to keep life as normal as it could be for her daughter. Sometimes Lauren would feel good enough to go to the playroom in the hospital. She liked to ride in the red wagon. Lisa pushed the IV pole behind.

Spring turned into summer turned into fall. Life was reduced to a 24/7 medical experience. In October came some of the hardest news of all. Statistics vary, but some show that as many as 80 percent of all couples with a severely sick child don't make it as a couple. That October, Brian filed for divorce.

Then came two more blows. The chemo had been going well, but white blood counts were still too high. Doctors were calling it a relapse. "That's a word you just never want to hear," Lisa said. Then in November, Lauren was diagnosed with still another form of cancer. This time, chemo and surgery wouldn't work. Lauren would need a bone marrow transplant.

"You have nothing to feel by then," Lisa said. "You're so beyond your emotional and mental capabilities. You don't know what to do or say. You're just screaming. You scream to be rescued. What more can you endure? I had nothing else to believe in besides God."

Lisa remembers praying specific prayers in the midst of that dark season. She put the burden back on God. If God promised that He would take care of people, then she was going to hold God to His promises. Not only that, but Lisa would pray for a miracle—no, three miracles:

She prayed for a healthy baby.

She prayed that her marriage would be restored.

She prayed that God would give her the amazing life He wanted her to have.

"I had big faith," Lisa said. "Big hope. Those were the cries of my heart."

WHEN YOU COME BACK

For the transplant, Lisa flew with Lauren to the Fred Hutchinson Cancer Research Center in Seattle, considered one of the top three bone marrow transplant hospitals in the world. No donor match was found, so doctors used stem cells donated from a little girl in St. Louis—not a perfect match, but the closest anyone could find. Before the transplant could occur, there needed to be more chemo and radiation to achieve what's considered 100 percent remission of the existing cancers.

On February 5, 2005, the stem cell transplant took place. It only took eleven minutes. Friends and family members held a little party in Lauren's hospital room, praying that the transplanted cells would do what they needed to do.

On Easter day, Lauren was released from the hospital, but she wasn't out of the woods yet. Lauren needed daily blood transfusions, as well as regular checks. Lisa and Lauren moved into an apartment near the hospital for three months. They went to the hospital every day. Lauren began to make progress. Soon they went to the hospital only every other day.

During that season, Lisa's nephew, eighth grader Jarrett Foote, started a Sparrow Club at his school. Lauren was adopted as a Sparrow. Students made cards, letters, and posters and did fund-raisers.

"It was great to have them participate with us and in Lauren's life," Lisa said. "We felt very supported."

By that July, Lauren was feeling much stronger. After fourteen months, her heart line was taken out. On August 1, they flew back to Florida. Tests confirmed that the transplant had "taken." Doctors began using the word *remission*.

"I used the word *healed*," Lisa explained. "God used those amazing physicians to heal her."

Another healing also took place.

Months earlier, after Lisa and Lauren had flown to the hospital in Seattle, Brian called up an old friend, a counselor. All the paperwork for the divorce had been done by then. All Brian had to do was sign his name. But the counselor encouraged him to wait to pick up the pen. Life is too short, the counselor said. You can't just quit in difficult times—otherwise you're alone.

In April, Brian flew to Seattle for Lisa's birthday.

In May, he flew out again for Lauren's birthday.

In June, he flew out for the couple's tenth anniversary.

In July he flew out one last time.

On that trip, Brian ripped up the divorce papers. When the family flew back to Florida on August 1, they flew together.

Not Just Any Pizza

I t starts with breast milk. Maybe some stewed peaches. Applesauce. Cream of Rice. Bits of bread. Swirled peas… Meal by meal, mouthful by mouthful, you taste, chew, swallow, and open wide again. Food is a whole new world to explore. Soon come bowlfuls of spaghetti, containers of yogurt, fruit bars, and chicken. Welcome to the world that helps you grow up strong.

When It's Hard to Even Eat

Right off the bat, Amy and Jerry Ulrey knew something was wrong with their baby. At one week old, little fair-skinned Tanner had blood in his stools. Maybe it was a milk allergy. No one seemed to know for sure.

Tanner also seemed to bruise very easily, even when he accidentally hit himself with a rattle. People thought it might just be because he was so fair. Others suspected something else. Amy received glares from people who saw bruises on Tanner. Amy formed a new appreciation for others who live with medical struggles of any kind. She quickly grasped the importance of not judging others just because they "look different" without really knowing what they've been through, she says. Then, at nine months old, Tanner hit his bottom teeth on the side of his highchair and bled for three days. Amy knew something was really wrong. Tanner wasn't eating like he should have either. In one three-month period, Tanner actually lost weight between checkups.

Amy had a cousin, Aaron, who had experienced something like this. The family has a history of Wiskott-Aldrich syndrome—a rare disorder that causes a low immune system and complications with the body's ability to absorb food. Recurrent infections, and a high risk for leukemia and lymph node tumors are typical. Aaron had had a bone marrow transplant, but died when he was sixteen. Amy tested negative as a carrier of the disease. Still she asked a doctor to run a platelet count for Tanner—the test that shows the disease.

Normal platelet counts range from 150,000–400,000. Tanner's were 37,000. Doctors thought it might be "a mild case" of Wiskott. Amy knew no such thing existed.

Tanner was going downhill fast. He had diarrhea all the time. Sometimes Amy found blood in his diaper. Sometimes he cried for up to eighteen hours a day. Being propped up on his daddy's shoulder was the only thing that would calm him down. The family went to a series of appointments. One hospital just sent Tanner home—they didn't know what to do. Another doctor put a feeding tube in. That night, Tanner slept for the first time in months.

With Wiskott-Aldrich syndrome, a person's body slowly breaks down. Tanner soon developed bad skin problems. His feeding tube had to be switched from nostril to nostril because the skin around his nose would break out in sores. Every other week, the tube would have to be taken out altogether so Tanner's nose could heal. At age two, a gastric tube was put in Tanner's stomach so he could get some food— any food. Amy noticed Tanner watching other children eating.

With a suppressed immune system, Tanner caught a bad bug that lodged in his stomach. Doctors could never really tell if the virus completely went away or if the virus had simply weakened his digestive system. Tanner's body would not digest or metabolize food. Finally, Tanner stopped eating all together.

HELP IS ON THE WAY

The family found an expert in Cincinnati and flew back for a consultation. The expert confirmed the course of action: A bone marrow transplant and chemotherapy was the only option. The family began to search for a donor. Three weeks later, a hospital found a perfect cord blood match. At age three, Tanner had the transplant. The family had insurance but ended up needing to live in Cincinnati for six months. Bills piled up.

Tanner was connected with a youth group in Oregon. The teens wrote letters and sent cards, held garage sales and car washes.

"You feel so alone when your child is sick," Amy says. "It was great to have so many people supporting us."

Tanner's transplant went well, but when he came home, he wasn't able to be around people for another six months. Isolation set in. Slowly he recovered. Sparrow Clubs helped with bills. But eating was still a problem.

Tanner would like certain foods—just to taste, but not to chew or swallow. Food still held such painful memories for him. His mom and dad tried everything—suckers, candy, anything to create new, positive associations with food. Nothing worked. Sometimes Tanner would pick something up and smell it, but he'd always put it down again. How do you get a little boy to eat when all he remembers of food is pain?

Then one day, just before Tanner started kindergarten, out of the blue he said, "Mom, I want a pepperoni pizza."

There was no immediate context for the request. Maybe Tanner had seen one on TV? Maybe he had seen one of his brothers or sisters eating one and thought it looked good?

It didn't matter. Amy rushed down to Little Caesars and picked one up. She brought it back to the house, cut a steaming slice, and set it on a plate before Tanner. Would the little boy eat?

Tanner picked up the pizza. He eyed the pepperoni. He sniffed along the crust. He licked the cheese.

Then he ate.

One slice.

One cautious slice.

One glorious slice of pepperoni pizza.

Tanner never looked back.

Today Tanner has joint pains and some food allergies, but he's doing well. He runs and plays. Girls fight over who gets to sit next to him at school lunches. His parents don't use the word *remission*; they use the word *cured*.

Amy and Jerry remember watching their son fall asleep each night when he was sick. He'd cry himself to sleep—his stomach hurt so badly that that was all he could do. Amy and Jerry used to cry too, then pray, then get up the next morning and do it all over again.

"I don't visit that place in my heart very often," Amy says. "I'm just happy he's alive."

A good day today involves playing catch in the front yard with Dad. Tanner and Jerry usually play with a Nerf football. Tanner has made up a team—the Barracudas. When he's eight, in two years, he says he's going to play for them. It's an imaginary team, but Tanner's got the name picked out anyway.

When Tanner and Jerry are done playing catch, they head inside the house. Amy serves up their favorite food—pepperoni pizza—as much as anyone wants to eat.

Everything I've Done Right

I n the old days, it would have been called reform school.
These days, they call it "a place of extended therapy." Call it
rehabilitation. Call it a place to get back on track. Bridges Boys
Academy is a live-in home for troubled youths in central Oregon.
It's not a lockup facility. The boys who go there don't wear striped
uniforms or work on chain gangs. Some are sent by parents. Others
are sent by the courts. A few have felonies and are sent to Bridges
instead of jail. Most are just regular kids who took the wrong path
in life.

Terminology doesn't matter so much to Jimmy Fargo, sixteen. All
he knows is that tomorrow he will graduate from Bridges Academy,
two months ahead of schedule.

And for that he's very happy.

THE OLD JIMMY

It all started during the summer after eighth grade. Jimmy started
smoking weed with his cousin. But problems ran deeper than that.
Life didn't make sense. It was hard to talk with his mom and dad.
Jimmy played the victim role a lot—*Why is all of this happening to*

me? He had no motivation for schoolwork. He refused to take responsibility for his actions. All he wanted to do was hang around with his friends and party.

Jimmy attended a Catholic school, where he first smoked weed with his friends, but for his ninth grade year, he switched to public school. It didn't take him long to find all the wrong friends again. In his new environment, he began to drink alcohol heavily and cut all the classes he could. He had several brushes with the law.

Eventually he was high "basically 24/7," Jimmy said. "Just to get through each day. I hated my parents. I'd go off the rails at the slightest thing. Everything was just screwed up, including me."

Jimmy came to what he describes as "a very dark place" in his life. He stayed there for months. Nobody in the family was talking. Jimmy's attitude was total defiance. His parents realized Jimmy was out of control. The final straw came after Jimmy had an intense argument with his dad and told him off.

Change began, severely, on a Monday in October at about 4:00 a.m.

Jimmy had gone to bed, high on drugs, about two hours earlier. When he woke up, two large men stood in his room. Handcuffs hung out of the pocket of one. Jimmy thought he was going to jail.

"Get up," one man said. "Get some clothes on."

Bleary-eyed and feeling sick, Jimmy didn't resist. He didn't know what was happening. A good thing, he said, because if he had known, he would have run away.

The men ushered Jimmy downstairs, where his parents stood beside the front door. No one said anything. His parents slowly turned away, crying. Jimmy's transporters took him to a white Crown Victoria and ordered him to get in. The child locks were set on the back doors so Jimmy couldn't jump out of the backseat. At one point he asked, "What's going on?"

"You're going to boarding school," was the only reply.

Jimmy slammed his head against the car window. After that, everything was fuzzy. The men took him to the Sacramento airport and flew with him that night to Bend, Oregon, to the Bridges Academy. Jimmy had never heard of it before. He had never heard of Bend, Oregon. He envisioned a *Shawshank Redemption*–style prison with brick walls and razor wire. In the early morning light, he saw the school clearly.

Instead of bars and barbed wire, Jimmy found a large, ranch-style facility in the high desert with a pool table and Ping-Pong. He was given new clothes—gray T-shirts and slacks. No logos. No affiliations. His new surroundings were much nicer than he'd expected, but he still couldn't believe the news: he would be here for the next twelve months. Jimmy felt shocked, sad, and angry, he said. When he found out how long he'd have to be there, he just put his head down on the table.

The first few weeks were pretty tough. Jimmy had to detoxify from all the drugs in his system and get used to having his own emotions again. Small things, like not being able to find a sheet of paper, could set him off. He went to regular workshops and counseling sessions. *Goal setting, skill mastery,* and *responsibility* became buzzwords. Outdoor exercise became a regular part of each day. For the first time, independence was seen as a privilege, not a right.

A Change of Direction

Part of what caused the change in Jimmy was a letter he wrote to his parents early in his stay at Bridges. Letter writing is part of the school's curriculum. The first letter, titled "Everything I've Done Wrong," is meant to be a confession, a clearing of the air, a beginning of an honest relationship between the parents and a child.

Writing that letter was one of the hardest things he'd ever done, Jimmy said. His was three single-spaced pages, typed in a small font. He read the letter to his parents over the phone. For one of the first times ever, he said, he realized how much he had hurt them. It was a turning point.

A few weeks later came a group discussion time. His parents flew up from Sacramento to participate. Jimmy felt as if he hadn't seen them in a long time. In that session, words were spoken that hadn't been spoken for years. Everybody laid it on the line. Everybody was bawling. "I told myself—and I told them—'I will never again be the person I once was,'" Jimmy said.

Another part of the change came as a result of the Sparrow program. Bridges had sponsored Michael, a teenager with a brain tumor. The kids from Bridges worked on fund-raisers and did community service projects to help.

"It was a real eyeopener," Jimmy said. "Michael's condition is terminal. He'll be dying within a year or so, but he's got a smile on his face. He's just enjoying life. I couldn't believe it."

Jimmy had the opportunity to meet Michael when he visited at the academy. The two played foosball together and hung out as friends. Jimmy described the face-to-face interaction with Michael as "short, but life changing."

"Beforehand I didn't know if he was able to walk or talk," Jimmy said, "but he looked like a normal teenager. He liked the same music I do. It was cool just to get to know him, hang out together, and have a conversation with him. Later that night, two guys got angry over who got in line first for dinner. I was like, 'Wow, we're getting mad over something so small.'"

Jimmy said Sparrow Club helped him realize it's good to help others before himself. He can wake up and not worry about the smaller things in life—who has the best car, who has the best clothes, who's ahead of him in line. Really, those things just don't matter as much.

"Life's not always about me anymore," he said.

A New Jimmy

Jimmy applied himself to the academy's curriculum. He took stock of his situation and decided to submit to his new surroundings. He rose to leadership levels early on in the program. Jimmy's been clean and sober for ten months now. His parents are visiting regularly, and everybody is getting along. The whole family's talking again.

"I've got a completely different perspective," Jimmy said. "I'm lucky and thankful for what my parents have done for me."

He has a plan in place to hang out with different friends when he goes home.

Spiritually, Jimmy once described his life as having "no faith," even though he was raised in a Catholic environment. "Basically, if I heard the word *God,* it'd make me mad," he said. "But now, with a clear head, I believe that where I am today couldn't have just *happened.* I know there's something more out there. It's about a relationship with God, not a religion."

A funny story happened while at the academy. One of the other students was a complete atheist. Jimmy used to just mess around with him by placing a huge Bible in his room when the guy was out. It used to drive the other guy nuts, he said. But one day Jimmy put the Bible in the guy's room and he started actually reading it. "Hey, this isn't too bad," the guy said.

"I don't know what that was all about," Jimmy said, "but it was kind of cool how it worked out in the end."

Jimmy plans to go to a technology high school when he gets back to Sacramento. He's not sure of his career choice yet, but he knows that school will be different.

One of the things he wants to do is begin a Sparrow Club at his new school. Before, he was never into school fund-raisers at all. He used to throw fliers advertising programs like that into the trash. But now he wants to be the first kid in his state to start a Sparrow Club.

"Life's different now," Jimmy said. "I'm going to graduate tomorrow and start over again. I know things are going to be different."

IF YOU GET CANCER

C ertain diseases can prompt certain mind-sets.

When Kim Kaiser was thirteen, her father died from cancer. He was an older man, sixty-three, and he had smoked. His disease began as oral cancer then spread to his lungs and his brain. Kim also witnessed several uncles die of the disease. Cancer just seemed a way of life in her family. It was like the ultimate pronouncement—if you got it, you were done. Kim's mom worked as a nurse, saw things up close, and always said she never wanted to go through treatment if she got the disease.

So Kim grew up thinking, *If you get cancer, you die.*

Maybe that's why she chose the profession she did. As a young adult, Kim completed a degree in health promotions and workplace wellness and got a job with the American Cancer Society, a nation-wide community-based voluntary health organization dedicated to eliminating cancer as a major health problem. The society provides information about cancer to schools and individuals, arranges fund-raisers for cancer research, and provides research grants to scientists looking for cures for the disease.

In a nutshell, Kim's employer aims to destroy cancer. That res-onated well with Kim.

Too Close to Home

Kim's private life took off as well. She and her husband, Chris, had two children, a boy, Tyler, and a little girl, Rylie. They settled in Billings, Montana, an all-American railroad city of about ninety thousand, surrounded by buttes and big sky. The future looked bright.

Rylie was always an active outdoorsy kid, but one month when she was almost four, she had a lot of low-grade fevers. She said her head hurt, and she spent a lot of time lying on the couch. The family had been traveling, and Kim thought it was perhaps a ploy for more attention. One Sunday Kim decided to take her daughter to a walk-in clinic, just to check. Tests looked fine. The doctor thought it was probably just a bug and prescribed antibiotics.

Two days later the clinic phoned. The blood work from Rylie's tests was done. All the caller said was, "You need to come in—right away."

At the clinic, the doctor started talking medical mumbo jumbo. He said it might be leukemia, but he wasn't sure. The family would need to fly to a larger hospital in Denver for a firm diagnosis. They should go right away.

Plane tickets on that short notice cost $2,000 apiece. Insurance wouldn't cover the tickets. Denver was nine hours away by car. Kim didn't think twice. She loaded Tyler and Rylie in the family car and headed out immediately. Her husband had just started a new job, so getting time off work was difficult for him. Kim thinks they would do things differently today; they would never have been apart when a child had medical problems. There's just too much stress on the relationship.

In the hospital in Denver, the diagnosis came back solid: Rylie had acute lymphoblastic leukemia. Kim's daughter had cancer. Kim had grown up always thinking that was a death sentence. She had dedicated her life to fighting the disease's existence. What would the family do?

The C-Word

Kim and Chris decided they would do everything possible to help save their daughter's life. Survival rates for Rylie's type of cancer are high—85–90 percent. Doctors mapped out a two-and-a-half-year treatment schedule, which Rylie began immediately.

The next seventeen months held all positive news. The treatment was aggressive at first, then became more maintenance. Tests all showed good counts, remission. Rylie only had to be hospitalized three times. (The family met another little girl with cancer at the hospital who was hospitalized fifteen times in the same time span.)

But then came a relapse, devastating news. Rylie was given a 40–50 percent chance of survival.

Rylie's body couldn't take another round of conventional chemotherapy, so a bone marrow transplant was the only option. The entire family drove back to Denver this time, but no family members were a match. The family researched the Fairview University Medical Center at the University of Minnesota, one of the pioneering hospitals of bone marrow transplants. The man who developed bone marrow transplants originally got a research grant from the American Cancer Society. Ironic that the company Kim works for helped save her daughter years before she was born.

Rylie ended up spending more than three months in the hospital in Minnesota, where she had a cord blood transplant and brain radiation. Once, Rylie needed to be isolated in her hospital room for twenty-eight days. Kim said it was a very difficult time for everybody.

Rylie had started kindergarten by that time, and her school started a Sparrow Club, which sponsored Rylie. Club members raised enough money so family members could fly to Minnesota to be with Rylie for part of the time. If not for the money raised, Rylie couldn't have seen her brother or father for nearly four months.

COMING HOME

Rylie was finally better enough to come home. But on the morning of the flight, Rylie was sick again. With three hours left to get their flight, Kim and Rylie got the call from the doctor that Rylie was well enough to take the flight. Mother and daughter rushed to the airport. After they were seated on the plane, a flight attendant talked to them for a bit, then said, "Why don't you come with me?" Kim and Rylie were upgraded to first class. When they landed, the waiting area was filled with friends and loved ones, cheering and waving signs, welcoming Rylie and Kim home. Rylie's room was filled with stuffed animals and gifts that people had sent.

Since then, all tests have come back good. Rylie's had her six-month checkup, her one-year checkup, and now her two-year checkup. Cancer hasn't been a death sentence for Rylie. Cancer has been beaten.

Today, at eight years old, Rylie is a pretty little girl with brown eyes and blond hair. She missed a year of school but is catching up. Rylie can do a cartwheel in gymnastics. Her mom describes her as a "real girly girl" who loves anything pink. Rylie has a pink soccer ball and a pink baseball glove. Recently the family, all Yankees fans, took in a Yankees-Twins game. Rylie took her baby doll, Charlie, to the game. Tyler, a huge baseball fan, rattled off stats on each player and described the various stances of each batter.

The Yankees won with three home runs. It was a good day for the Kaiser family.

THE CURE

From about fifth grade on, Lindsay McPhail had an eating disorder—a tangled combination of bulimia and compulsive exercise. She went on antidepressants. She went to therapy. When she graduated high school, the disorder was still with her. A friend had a connection to an international relief organization in Santiago, Chile, the country's capital and largest city. Lindsay took a chance, flew down, and for six months worked in a soup kitchen for street kids in one of the worst quarters of the city. While there she fed rice and chicken to hungry kids; she played ball and hopscotch; she combed bugs out of the kids' hair. At the end of six months, Lindsay's eating disorder was gone.

"I needed to look beyond myself," she said. "That cured me."

WHEN YOU LOOK OUT FOR OTHERS

During those six months in Chile, Lindsay said, a new, lifelong pattern was established for her. Life became about helping others and giving back to people. She went to college and married a youth pastor, a young man intent on the same goals. Together they worked for a large church in southern Oregon. At the church was the largest indoor skateboard facility in the region. It became a community center of sorts for all the kids in the area, whether from churched backgrounds or not. The church became a place of safety and sanctuary—it didn't matter what a kid had been into. Many nights the church drew quite a rough crowd.

Lindsay and her husband hoped to introduce the kids they worked with to issues larger than themselves, so they took their kids on international service trips to Mexico. The students met other kids who lived and worked in migrant camps. Many American students saw life beyond affluence for the first time.

But as crazy as it sounds, even trips to Mexico can become routine to students. There's sort of an initial "high" when a student comes back home, Lindsay said. He or she often wants to change the world for a few weeks. But familiarity beckons, and students can easily slip back into old patterns of ungratefulness, selfishness, and materialism.

What their youth ministry needed was a more lasting vehicle to help students learn how to look beyond themselves.

When You See Change

Lindsay remembers the night her husband introduced the high school students to Tanner, a three-year-old boy with a blood disorder whom the youth group had adopted as a Sparrow child. Tanner came to the youth meeting with his mom, Amy. He needed a bone marrow transplant. The disease had taken its toll on him. He looked pretty beat up. Amy and her son routinely attended the church and knew some of the kids. Lindsay's husband asked her if some of the kids could pray for Tanner.

After he made the request, Lindsay's husband had second thoughts about what he had done. His youth group kids were not known for being overt pray-ers. Most weren't "churchy" kids. They didn't sing worship songs. They were skaters. Raw street kids. Some had been caught having sex in a back room at the church. Some were into drugs.

But Amy agreed, and Lindsay's husband invited the youth group kids to pray. He closed his eyes not knowing what would happen.

"It was absolutely amazing," Lindsay said. The normally rough crowd of two hundred high school students sat quietly for a moment, then kids began to pray. In front of their skater friends, kids got on their knees. Others raised their hands. Some lay flat on the floor, unaccustomed to the intensity of the moment but praying anyway—as hard as they could. The entire room was engulfed in prayer.

"A huge shift happened that night in our youth group," Lindsay said. "Our kids felt something for this little guy. They knew it was beyond their power. They had nowhere to look but to God."

From then on, the youth group climate was changed. Barriers were broken. Kids who normally clashed got along. The youth group rallied their efforts around the little boy with a blood disorder.

And Tanner made a full recovery.

Soon, Lindsay and her husband joined Sparrow Clubs as staff members. Lindsay worked as a program coordinator. She remembers driving to the first school assembly she had to speak at. She was so nervous that she prayed she would get into a car accident so she wouldn't have to speak in public. That was twenty assemblies ago. "I still don't like public speaking," Lindsay says with a grin. "But at least I know I can do it."

Over the years, the McPhails have seen hundreds of kids' lives changed for the better. Consistently, they see students learn to view life beyond themselves. Students learn compassion, hope, and how to care for others in need. There are moments of victory and triumph and moments of heartache. Going to funerals is a consistent and aching part of the job.

But the stories of good far outweigh the bad.

There was Miles, a six-year-old with a bad heart, whom Lindsay describes as "a giant of a boy." His mom was a bit skeptical of Sparrow Clubs at first because she was bent on proving that her son was like every other kid. Then Miles needed open-heart surgery. He was adopted as a Sparrow, and a high school cheered him on. The mom began to open up, to receive help and love.

There was the mother of a healthy kid, whose son had volunteered to help with Sparrow Clubs. The student had had some problems in school before. After a few months the mom phoned. "I don't know what you've done, but you've changed my son," she said.

"It's an emotional job for sure," Lindsay says, with a smile. "But I love it. In many ways, we've been able to minister more now that we've left church work than when we were there. Sparrow Clubs is a challenge every day. It forces you to grow, to trust, and to look beyond yourself. I just wish I had known about Sparrow Clubs earlier. Maybe then I wouldn't have needed to go to Chile."

Two Minutes Between the Veil

E li Golden was born dead.

His mom, Theresa Golden, had been scheduled for a C-section at 5:00 a.m. on a Monday. But at 4:00 p.m. the day before, her water broke. Blood was in the water. After rushing to the emergency room, Theresa learned the umbilical cord was tightly wrapped around the baby's neck three times. No anesthesiologist was on duty that day, just an EMT who fed Theresa morphine and Demerol. Theresa was awake when the emergency surgeon started cutting.

She remembers thinking, *This is really going to stink.* She doesn't remember anything after that.

"Don't Write Him Off"

Eli Golden was born dead.

The baby was gray and pasty. His Apgar score—the one to ten rating for a newborn's health—was *zero*.

For husband, Jon, and big sister, Alli, the news looked grim.

Several years later, Theresa and Jon bumped into the emergency room doctor who had delivered Eli. He recognized them.

"Do you remember the baby who was born dead a couple years ago?" Theresa asked him.

"I think about you guys all the time," the doctor said. "I only see the bad, never the good. I never knew how it turned out, but I know that in cases like yours, usually neither the mother nor the child survive."

"Guess what…" Theresa said.

At birth, the baby had no pulse. No breathing. No responsiveness. Nothing. Then came two anxious minutes of speed and ferocity—two minutes between the veil—and the medical team revived Eli Golden. What would happen after that nobody could say for sure.

Eli gasped to life, kicking and screaming. Seizures—screaming, convulsing, five-minute-long seizures. He was stabilized in an incubator, then taken by a Life-Flight helicopter to a children's hospital some three hours away, where the seizures continued. Doctors weren't sure if the little baby's brain was going to connect. It took Theresa three days before she was well enough to make the drive over to be with her child. She remembers looking at their tiny son in the midst of a spasm, the child twisting in pain.

"Do you think we should've revived him?" Theresa whispered to Jon.

"Yeah," Jon said. Just one word. Theresa agreed—she just wanted to make sure. That was all the couple ever said about it.

The hospital where Eli stayed was a teaching hospital. Professors came around and discussed diagnoses with groups of students. Theresa remembers asking one doctor what the quality of her son's life would be. The doctor didn't know. Theresa cried at that point. She had been crying a lot. But the doctor said one thing that Theresa filed away—one thing that kept her going in the season when parents are in such tremendous uncertainty:

"Babies are resilient," the doctor said. "Don't write him off."

When Kids Are Superheroes

The Goldens were told that Eli would need to be in the hospital for months. But after two weeks, the child was stable enough to come home. There was no concrete diagnosis for the seizures. Nothing solid was given to help predict his future. But he was well enough to leave the hospital despite a feeding tube that went through his nose into his tummy. The Goldens would take it as a good sign.

Months passed, and the baby grew. His muscles were stiff, he couldn't sit up at the same time as others in his age group, and he couldn't eat on his own. The Goldens got involved in an early intervention program right away. Still, they knew something was wrong. When Eli turned one, doctors confirmed cerebral palsy.

"I'm not complaining," Theresa said. "It could have been much worse. But it's hard because it's your baby. You only want the best for your kid."

There are five levels of cerebral palsy, with level 5 being the most severe. Eli is level 2. Now at age three, his muscles are looser and he can walk. Fine motor skills are hard though. For instance, it's difficult for Eli to move a fork into his mouth. But cognitively he's completely normal. He's very bright actually—even above where he should be. He's developed a sly sense of humor. When he met his teacher at early intervention, she introduced herself as "Miss Kitty."

Miss Kitty, thought Eli. *How could she be a cat?* "No-o-o-o-o-o," he said wisely.

Eli's current favorites are knock-knock jokes. He makes them up himself.

Eli: Knock knock.

Mom: Who's there?

Eli: Banana-head.

Mom: Banana-head who?

Eli: Banana-head, banana-head! Ha ha ha ha ha!!!

Through the early intervention program, the Goldens learned about Sparrow Clubs. At first they were hesitant. "There are so many kids worse off than us," Theresa said. But club representatives insisted. "This is what we do," they told her.

"It's very humbling, to receive," Theresa said. "It puts you on a whole new level. You become so grateful, so undeserving…so blessed."

Eli was adopted by Evergreen Elementary in Redmond, Oregon. The school poured out love and encouragement. Kids helped the family in droves—a school of young superheroes in action. Right away, the school held a jump-a-thon. The little boy who won received a $100 gift certificate for toys. He made his wish list, then erased it and gave his gift certificate to Eli. The school also held a tea party for big sister, Alli—they wanted to make sure she felt included. At the tea party, the schoolgirls gave Alli a dolly. Alli named her new dolly Sparrow.

The club raised enough money for Eli to receive equestrian therapy. After two weeks of riding on a therapy horse, Eli could hold a crayon in his hand and was able to color with his big sister—he had never been able to do so before. A year after the therapy began, Eli returned to the school for another assembly. He was able to walk much better than he could before.

"It was great for the kids to see that—the results of what they had done," Theresa said. "Something they did helped a little boy walk better. When kids can do something for someone else, they're so excited, so happy. I want every school in the nation to be involved in Sparrow Clubs."

The future is still unknown for Eli Golden, but his mom and dad are confident he'll be able to do much.

Just today, Eli put on his Batman cape and went outside to play with his friends. His cape has lightning flashes on it. When Eli wears the cape, he feels like a superhero too, his mom says.

Not bad for a little guy who once spent two minutes between the veil.

Not bad at all.

SPARROWS OF JOY

It gives me that good old fuzzy feeling to think that we're helping shape this child's life through our efforts.

—SPARROW CLUB MEMBER, HIGH SCHOOL AGE

OUR FATHER'S HOUSE

It was years ago. Linda McCoy's son Daniel had just heard the Audio Adrenaline song "Big House." He came running out to the front yard where Linda was puttering in a flower bed.

"Mom!" Daniel said. "You've got to hear this!

"Come and go with me, to my Father's house.

It's a big, big house, with lots and lots of rooms."*

When Linda heard the song, she cried. "That was exactly where my heart was," Linda says. "To have a big, big house with lots and lots of rooms someday—a big house that belongs to the Father."

Linda and her husband, Mike, prayed that their dream would come true. They envisioned a sprawling house out in the country, the most kid-friendly house around—with swing sets and a big grassy yard. Maybe they'd turn the garage into a music room someday. And no gates either! With gates, you have to worry about someone leaving one open and a kid wandering out. With no gates, everyone just watches everyone, and you don't have to worry.

Filling a big, big house would not be a problem.

---

* Lyrics excerpt from Audio Adrenaline, "Big House," *Don't Censor Me.* Composers Barry Blair, Bob Herdman, Mark Stuart, Will McGinniss. Copyright © 1993 by Forefront.

MEET THE McCOY FAMILY

When asked to name all her children today, Linda McCoy finds it easier to simply hand you a list. There's Heidi (now married to Dr. Kevin Limbaugh), Daniel (married to Caitlyn Barnes McCoy), Shelly (married to Jeremy Denton), Leah, Eli, Elizabeth, Augustine, Zack, Shellee, Patrick, Brooklynn, and Brianna.

Four are biological. Eight are adopted. There have been others, too. Over the years, the McCoys have housed more than fifty children through fostering and adoption programs. These days, with nine children still at home, the McCoys' dishwasher runs four times daily. The family does six loads of laundry each day of the week. Other homes are decorated Colonial style or Craftsman. The McCoys joke that their house is decorated "Early American Yard Sale." About the only new piece of furniture they've ever bought is a ten-foot oak dining table. That way, every morning at 7:00, the whole family can sit down together for breakfast. The McCoys wouldn't want it any other way.

"We just love kids," Linda says. "Lots of kids. It's our calling."

Mike and Linda had an unusual calling from the start. At ages forty-eight and forty-three, they've been married for twenty-seven years. Yep, do the math. They were married at ages twenty-one and sixteen.

"I was jailbait," Linda says with a grin.

But their marriage was much more purposeful than that. Linda and Mike both grew up in rural Idaho. Linda had been dating Mike's younger brother, but when he joined the Navy, things cooled off and Linda began to date Mike. Mike already ran a dairy farm. He didn't need a schoolgirl. He needed a wife and business partner. Also speeding up the time line was Linda's father, terminally ill with cancer. Linda wanted to get married before he passed away. So Linda quit high school, got her GED, and Mike and Linda tied the knot. It wasn't a shotgun wedding, as everyone supposed. Neighbors counted the months with a watchful eye, but the McCoys' first child was born thirteen months later. *See, we were telling the truth!*

Three years after Number One, Number Two came right on schedule. Three years after Two came Three. The perfect family. Linda and Mike were done. By the time Three was all set for first grade, Linda was set to start college herself. Time for a career. Whoops, Number Four was born, surprising everybody. Well, okay, college can wait for a while. Linda phoned a nearby pregnancy center to donate all her maternity clothes. She wouldn't need *those things* anymore.

The woman on the other end of the phone at the pregnancy center had a strange sound in her voice. Not bad, just contemplative. Linda had met her a few times before. They were friends even. A few minutes after Linda hung up, the phone rang. It was the same woman from the center.

"Uh, I know this is totally crazy," the woman began, "but we've just had a fourteen-year-old come to us pregnant, with nowhere to live. Think she would be able to stay with you guys for a while?"

It was one of those instant decisions, Linda remembers. She didn't even think to say no.

So fourteen-year-old Lina came to live with the McCoy family until the baby was born. Linda took Lina to all her doctor appointments. She coached the birth. In the end, Lina asked the McCoys to adopt her child. Linda's own son Eli was just one year and two weeks old. A pediatrician suggested that the best thing for the new baby, a girl named Elizabeth, was to have Linda nurse her along with Eli. Linda agreed. That baby, Lizzie, is twelve years old today and is a beautiful child. Lina still comes to visit.

And that started it all.

MORE KIDS, MORE FUN...

Linda and Mike first saw Patrick's picture in a brochure put out by an adoption agency. The pamphlet described a shy, warm, fun four-year-old who was sweet, lovable, and quiet. Patrick had been born to mentally ill parents, who had problems taking care of him. The brochure also mentioned he was "a special child with an unknown future." Patrick has Goldenhar syndrome—a congenital birth defect that can often lead to deformities on one side of the face. He was missing most of his right ear but could hear out of his left. Patrick also has agenesis of the corpus callosum—another rare birth defect in which the structure that connects the two hemispheres of the brain is partially or completely absent. "Only time will tell what Patrick will face in life," the brochure read.

Linda and Mike weren't put off by the description. They were no strangers to adoption by then and knew this was a child probably no one would want. They also knew that prognoses could be hugely off target. One of their other children, Shellee, had come with a heart defect when she was adopted. The McCoys were told she'd always be profoundly retarded and would never be able to walk or talk. Shellee is six years old today and runs all over the place while babbling up a storm.

"You just never know what a kid can do," Linda says. "With love, faith, and prayer, if someone really believes in them and helps them meet their goals, who knows what they can do!"

The McCoys adopted Patrick. One twist—just before the McCoys saw the brochure for Patrick, they had looked into adopting twins, Brooklynn and Brianna. The twins had been born prematurely at twenty-three weeks; both weighed well under two pounds at birth. Brianna developed cerebral palsy. The McCoys wanted the girls, now age four, but complications in the foster care system had prevented the children's placement. The McCoys were saddened but accepted that a stronger plan was at work.

Unbeknown to anybody, the twins' grandparents were praying that the girls would still be adopted. A short time after Patrick was placed, the phone rang. The foster care worker was breathless. Incredible hurdles had just been overcome in the twins' paperwork. Did the McCoys still want the girls?

"Absolutely," came the reply.

In the Big, Big House

"I pray for Patrick," Linda says. "I pray he will grow up to have a sound mind."

Adopting a special needs child can be an incredible experience, Linda says, but it is seldom easy. Patrick will need reconstructive surgery on his ear. It will cost about $30,000 and, for some reason, isn't covered by insurance. Mike has a good job with a school district, but it's still a lot for the family. The McCoys receive some money for taking care of foster children, but when children are adopted, the amount goes down by as much as half. Still, the McCoys believe adoption is best for all of the children they care for. They believe in the security that a sense of permanency brings to a child.

Two elementary schools have adopted Patrick as their Sparrow. Patrick will attend one this fall as a first grader. Raising $30,000 isn't the goal. More so, it's to support and encourage the McCoys, to get to know Patrick, and to welcome him to the school. Patrick has already visited several times.

Linda looks upon Sparrow Clubs with gratefulness. She speculates that without Sparrow, in the largely Caucasian community in which the McCoys live, Patrick (who is black) would have been known at school as "the little black kid with one ear."

"But now he's a *Sparrow,*" Linda says, emphasizing the word proudly. "It's made a big difference in how Patrick is perceived. He's protected, defended, known, liked."

And Patrick is doing well in his new surrounds in the McCoy house. Because he only has one ear, sometimes he doesn't hear things correctly. Other times, his new mom thinks, he hears them exactly but just makes a family game out of it. For example, Patrick has a friend, Alison, whom he calls "Ell-i-fell-ant" (sound it out to get the full effect). Awhile ago Mike asked him to go get a *pair of pliers.* "Air pliers?" said Patrick. "What are air pliers?"

Most days, Patrick is all about fun. A few days after he celebrated a recent birthday, a car knocked out an electrical transformer in the area, resulting in a power outage. Linda lit some candles, and Patrick figured it was time to celebrate again. He sang "Happy Birthday" to himself and blew the candles out. When the power finally came back on, Patrick celebrated by singing and doing a little dance around the kitchen:

"We got power!

We got the power on, oh yeah!"

The kitchen is in the McCoys' big, big house.

They bought it awhile back. It's a sprawling eight-bedroom, four-bathroom ranch style located on five acres—one of the most kid-friendly properties you could find anywhere. There's a big swing in the living room. Mike and Linda turned the garage into a music room. And outside are nothing but grassy fields—no gates—the best place ever for a kid to play.

THAT'S KINDA COOL

S pencer Brennan, fifteen, a high school sophomore, isn't one for many words. He likes video games, hanging out with his friends, and well, just cool stuff. But Spencer's life would change in ways he could never imagine. In the end, he learned something about what's truly important in life…

A FAKER OR WHAT?

When Spencer was in sixth grade, he was just like any other kid, active and healthy. Most important to him was making as many friends as possible. His stomach used to hurt a lot though. Like on the first day of school, it hurt so bad he could hardly go. Maybe it was just nerves. His big sister called him a faker. Problem was, Spencer liked school. He wasn't scared to go at all. Something was wrong.

Spencer had never been in the hospital before. At first he was told he had cancer, but it turned out to be necrobacillosis—a bunch of pockets of bacteria in his stomach, not tumors at all. It was still serious. Surgeons took out Spencer's spleen. He was in the hospital for three months—all tubes and stuff. His friends stuck by him.

They'd call him up and tell him about video games and just say, "Hey, we're prayin' for ya." Stuff like that. Spencer passed the time at the hospital by e-mailing friends. He kept up with his school-work at the hospital's school. When Spencer was better enough to come home, he still had a tutor for a while. Then he went back to school.

That year, sixth grade for Spencer, the school had sponsored a Sparrow child, a little girl named McKenzie. Her parents were in the middle of building a new house when their child got sick. Plans were put on hold. Spencer joined the Sparrow Club and went out with his friends and picked up wood at the construction site to help the parents out.

"I just figured I should help out," Spencer said. "Maybe I could help get the family's spirits up."

The following summer, McKenzie died. It was sad, Spencer said, really sad, but he still felt as if he had at least done something. The following year, he signed up for Sparrow Club again. That year his school sponsored a little boy with leukemia. The boy's family lived close to the school, and Spencer would see the boy out walking with his mom. Whenever they passed, Spencer would always wave and say hi. The boy and his mom would always wave back.

He joined Sparrow Club in eighth grade too. Then, when he started high school the following year, he joined Sparrow Club again. High school is more about grades than junior high ever was, he says, but his goals haven't changed. He still wants to help out wherever he can.

THAT'S KINDA COOL

Awhile back, Spencer's school held several fund-raisers for their Sparrow child. Spencer figured he could raise a lot of money. So he really went for it. He ended up raising $1,000 all by himself.

At the end of the year, the school held an awards assembly. This lady came up and had a trophy. She started talking about how one kid had really outdone himself. Then she looked right at Spencer. She called his name. Spencer had won the Dameon Award for outstanding service, a trophy given in honor of the boy who started Sparrow Clubs.

"I felt happy," Spencer said. "My friends were all like, 'Wow, that's kinda cool.'"

A Beautiful Plan

Tami Farrell never dreamed that by age eighteen she would've traveled all over the world, raised $21 million for charity, and helped a nonprofit organization jump to national prominence. But she did.

An unlikely life event helped her on that road: as a junior high student, she got sick.

Tomboy Roots

Tami had always been a go-getter, an athlete, and a star pupil in school. With one older brother and one younger brother, Tami had grown up competitive and a bit of a tomboy, she admits. Life was all about being as good as the boys. As a kid she played soccer, basketball, baseball, softball, and ran track. Wearing a dress or putting on lipstick was the furthest thing from her mind.

One day when she was about twelve, Tami was at her grandma's house and passed out. Nobody quite knew why. A series of doctor visits began, with no concrete diagnosis. A year later, Tami passed out at a soccer game. Her condition slowly intensified. Once, when watching a movie with family, Tami was overcome with chest pains and shortness of breath. More doctor visits. Still no answer. Sports became a struggle, but Tami was stubborn. She wore a heart monitor at track meets. Then seizures began her sophomore year. Something would definitely have to change. Finally, she was diagnosed with vasovagal syncope—essentially the electrodes in her heart go haywire, which makes her dizzy and likely to pass out. She was also diagnosed with an irregular heartbeat and a small, benign brain tumor in the center of her brain.

Not much could be done. She'd get checked each year for the brain tumor, and well, for the heart problems—*simply slow down.*

Tami sighs when she tells the story. She almost chuckles.

"I sound like a soap opera," she says. "The thing is, all this landed right around the age when you're figuring out who you are and who you want to be. I was always known as an athlete—that was all I was ever good at. Now that was gone. Who was I now?"

Despite the diagnosis, Tami tried to keep up with sports. She switched to cheerleading, even though it really wasn't her thing. She felt uncoordinated and "out in left field." One morning at cheer practice, Tami was having a hard time keeping up. She felt out of breath, dizzy, and her heart pounded. When the coach suggested a break, all the blood rushed out of Tami's face, her lips turned blue, and she passed out. She was rushed to the emergency room. She cheered at one more competition, but event coordinators made sure paramedics were on hand—just for Tami.

"It felt pretty embarrassing," she said. "That was the end of cheerleading for me."

MISS CONGENIALITY

Tami was student body president her senior year of high school. One of her responsibilities involved assemblies, which were always poorly attended. When a friend, Joni Mahon, suggested the school become involved with Sparrow Clubs, Tami thought it was a bird club at first. But Tami researched the program, went to a conference, and introduced Sparrow Clubs to her school. She held a series of assemblies, word spread about the club, and attendance and involvement grew.

The school's first Sparrow child was a young girl named Paige. Paige had beautiful pale skin, amazing blue eyes, and just like Tami, a heart condition. They formed an instant bond. Other students also fell in love with the little girl, who became a permanent fixture at a variety of school functions.

"It was crazy," Tami said. "The students who you'd never think would help were often the first to sign up. Paige just had an incredible impact on us all."

At the start of her senior year, Tami entered a pageant, mostly just to see what she could do, and won the Miss Teen Oregon competition. Tami was quite surprised at the results. She was a jock—and an unhealthy jock at that. "I just wasn't the pageant type," she said.

That spring when she graduated, Tami entered the Miss Teen USA pageant—with fifty of the most beautiful, talented girls in the nation, all with public service résumés the length of their arms. Tami was sure she'd never go far in the competition, but her mom pointed her to a higher source.

"Just go have fun and shine," her mom told her. It was an invitation to see the pageant spiritually. God had a plan for Tami's life, and if that meant winning a pageant for some larger purpose, it was all in His hands.

Tami prayed and decided to give the pageant her best shot. She flew to Palm Springs, California, for the event. After two weeks, the field of fifty was narrowed to the top fifteen.

Tami remembers the count well. *Three, four, five…* She stood with the other girls as names were called one by one. *Six, seven, eight…* Each girl was so amazing, so beautiful. Tami knew she'd never make it. *Twelve, thirteen, fourteen…* Only one spot left. Surely it would never be her. From the stage, Tami looked out at her mother in the audience. Mom was pointing up. Tami understood the meaning: "Trust God."

When the fifteenth girl was called, Tami couldn't believe her ears. *Tami Farrell.* It was her. Tami was the last girl picked.

"It was completely overwhelming," Tami said. "I started crying. Making the top fifteen felt like winning the whole competition to me."

The pageant continued. When the top ten were called, Tami was ninth picked, and when the top five were called, Tami was third.

It all came down to this. There she was, one of only three girls vying for the crown of Miss Teen USA. Tami was sure she wouldn't make it, but one thing sealed her fate for sure. She had always joked with friends that winning the title of "Miss Congeniality" was the kiss of death in any pageant. The title is an honor, Tami knew, as it is the one award that is picked by all the other girls, not the judges. It goes to the girl most liked and respected.

When Tami was called for Miss Congeniality, she felt honored and sad at the same time. She knew Miss Congeniality never wins.

Curtain Call

This time, Miss Congeniality surprised them all.

Tami Farrell, the one-time tomboy, ex-jock, ex-cheerleader with a heart condition, won Miss Teen USA 2003. Music played and the crowd roared as the crown was set on her head. Tami had done it.

That night was a flurry of activity and interviews. After a short night of sleep, Tami met with pageant representatives early the next morning. In a few hours she would be flying to New York City to begin her year's reign and responsibilities as Miss Teen USA. It was then that something amazing happened. Every winner speaks throughout the year on the platforms of self-confidence and drug and alcohol awareness. Tami asked if she could speak on those and add a third platform, the one that had meant so much to her in high school: Sparrow Clubs USA. Pageant officials researched the program and gave their approval—not only for Tami, but for every Miss Teen USA after her. Sparrow Clubs became the third official platform of the pageant.

That year, Tami spoke around the nation and around the world. She visited children's hospitals. She spoke at openings, programs, schools, and public-service venues everywhere. Because of her,

Sparrow Clubs' influence went from a regional to a national charity, almost overnight. Countless more sick and disabled children and their families were touched for the better. Countless more schools and youth clubs were changed through sponsoring Sparrow children.

"It was totally a God thing," Tami said. "If I had never gotten sick and quit sports, I never would have done pageants. You just have to trust God and His beautiful plan."

JUST LIVING THROUGH THE MIDDLE

On the front cover of Amy Hayes's medical binder are these words: *Once upon a Time...*

The binder contains years' worth of information: every medical record, every prescription, every doctor's contact information, every scrap of history. Amy's mom, Debbie, made the binder when Amy first got sick. Debbie chose a pink binder—her daughter's favorite color.

Debbie wrote a message on the back of the binder too. She knew the ending already; the family just had to live through the middle first.

THE FRONT OF THE BINDER...

Once upon a time, there lived a high school sophomore who loved the color pink. The sophomore grew up in Indiana and had always been healthy and active. She loved cheerleading, dance, and softball. For a few weeks she'd had a pain in her rib cage—probably just a pulled muscle from softball practice. But the pain continued through the season. It even got worse. Amy felt it every time she took a breath.

X-rays were taken. Doctors didn't see anything, but one savvy radiologist noticed a "shadow." He was just curious; maybe it was a calcium deposit. Mom tried hard to keep the situation very calm. A CAT scan showed some sort of growth pushing into Amy's chest wall. Surgery was done to remove it. Everything went smoothly.

Amy was out Rollerblading with a friend when the surgeon phoned with the biopsy results. When Amy came home, her mom was talking faster than usual, almost panicky—some story about a friend who knew someone…who… *It didn't quite make sense,* Amy thought. Debbie sent Amy out for some more Rollerblading. What Debbie really needed to do was phone the doctor back for more information. When Amy came back the second time, Debbie sat her down.

"We need to talk," mother said to daughter. Her voice was straightforward. Her daughter had a right to know. "You have cancer."

Amy burst into tears. She wondered if she was going to die. Then she had another horrible thought, for a sophomore girl almost more horrible than the first. She had always had beautiful blond hair—it hung past her lower back. *What would happen to her hair?*

THE MIDDLE OF THE BINDER…

The news was not good—Ewing's sarcoma, bone cancer. But it could have been worse. Survival rates were 75 percent, well on the positive side. Amy, Debbie, dad Bill, and younger daughter Lindsay never dreamed of anything other than a full recovery.

Treatments came fast and consistent: two surgeries, ten rounds of chemotherapy, ten months of misery. School started that fall, and Amy went, cancer or no cancer. Some friends understood; some didn't. Complications set in. Nerves in Amy's feet grew tingly. Her walking became affected. One nerve in her face made her left eye droop.

Then what Amy had feared from the start happened. It happened in the hospital, all in one day. That morning Amy's head itched. Her mom began to brush her hair, which made her head feel better. Mom knew what was really going on. She wouldn't let her daughter see until it was all over. Amy's beautiful hair was gone. That evening, they came home and had a party—a pool luau with a bunch of friends. Amy's dad shaved his head for his daughter so they'd be bald together. Amy wore a bright pink bandanna—her favorite color.

"I think I grew up a lot that year," Amy said. "You learn what's truly important and what isn't."

Lindsay and a cousin, Bailey Voss, were in third and fourth grade at the same elementary school. They decided to do something. An aunt had heard of Sparrow Clubs via the Internet. Lindsay and Bailey began a Sparrow Club for Amy. Fund-raisers were held; support flooded in.

And the year continued.

By the next summer, the treatment had run its course, and Amy was feeling a lot better. The battle looked over. Amy picked up with dance and cheer. But at the beach one day with friends, she felt totally exhausted. She knew something wasn't quite right. She remembers the nurse crying when she told Amy the news. The nurse started off by saying, "I don't quite know how to tell you this..."

Amy's cancer was in remission. But because of the harshness of the chemotherapy, Amy had developed myelodysplastic syndrome, a precursor to leukemia. The initial "cure" had been so hard on her body that it had healed the original disease, but caused another one in its wake.

Surprisingly, the family greeted the news with resiliency. "We weren't as upset this time," Amy said. "It was like, 'We did this once; we can do it again.'"

But the second malady was no simple disease. The only option was a bone marrow transplant. Primary family members were tested, but none was a match. Amy was put on the registry for the national bone marrow donor program. The wait began.

A good match was found in just a few months, fairly quick in the cancer world. But by that time, the disease had turned into leukemia. That January 17, Amy turned seventeen. She celebrated her golden birthday at an ice-skating party with friends. Then she went and had a bone marrow transplant.

The transplant was considered a success, but complications set in. Amy developed an intestinal infection. Her stomach hurt so bad she couldn't eat or drink anything for five weeks. Doctors gave her a 40 percent chance of survival. Debbie kept adding pages to the binder.

Once, after Amy had been in the hospital for nearly a month, Lindsay was missing her older sister very much. The worst of Amy's infection was over by then, and the girls' parents surprised Lindsay with a special treat. Dad packed all her stuff in secret, saying it was just a visit. But when Lindsay got to the car, Dad told her it was going to be a sleepover in the hospital—just Lindsay and Amy. Amy cries when she tells the story today.

"My little sister was so excited to spend the night at the hospital with me," Amy says. "Can you believe it? The hospital is usually the last place any kid wants to be. I was so proud of her—all the way through it, she was just incredible."

That night the girls watched videos, played Scattergories and drew pictures on a huge dry-erase board on a wall in the hospital—flowers, hearts, and tick-tack-toe. Both girls say it was one of the best times together they've ever had.

The Back of the Binder...

Today, Amy, twenty-one, is a senior at Indiana University, majoring in human development/family studies. She plans to work as a child life specialist in a children's hospital. Lindsay, fifteen, is a fun-loving, clothes-borrowing little sister. Debbie and Bill are both doing well. Amy's been cancer-free for several years now. Both cancers are considered gone.

"Most people don't even get one miracle in their lifetime," Debbie said. "We got two."

Amy is active in a sorority at her university. She organizes fund-raisers for cancer research organizations. She also volunteers in the hospital playroom at the University of Chicago Comer Children's Hospital. As sick children gear up for surgery, Amy gives them encouragement and plays with them—video games for older kids usually, finger paints for the younger ones. Some of the patients she works with know what she's been through; some don't. Mostly, Amy's experience comes out through her listening. Colleagues say she has an uncanny way of setting sick children's hearts at ease.

And Amy's pink binder? The one with the front cover that reads *Once upon a Time...*?

The message on the back cover sums it up well. Debbie wrote it there the same day her daughter got sick. She refused to think of the low points that were to come. She only ever dreamed of one conclusion.

And They Lived Happily Ever After...

All they had to do was live through the middle.

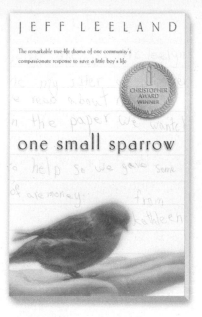

RESTORE YOUR FAITH

Read the poignant true story behind the founding of Sparrow Clubs U.S.A. Jeff Leeland shares the tragedy-to-triumph story of his infant son's leukemia diagnosis and how the generous spirit of one junior high student inspired a whole community to contribute to Leeland's cause.

About Sparrows Clubs USA

Proceeds from sales of *A Thousand Small Sparrows* benefit Sparrow Clubs USA, the non-profit organization behind the stories in this book. Sparrow Clubs assist kids in schools and communities to perform simple yet heroic acts of kindness which help kids in medical crisis. The mission of Sparrow Clubs is supported by caring individuals and companies. Gifts to the organization are 100% tax-deductible. To learn more about Sparrows Clubs and how you can get involved, visit www.sparrowclubs.org.

Available in bookstores and from online retailers.

Multnomah

Keeping Your Trust…One Book at a Time
www.mpbooks.com